THE ANCIENT EASTERN MEDITERRANEAN

Papers presented at a symposium
to celebrate
the **centennial year of**
the Chicago Society of
the Archaeological Institute of America

March 31, 1990
Edited by
Eleanor Guralnick

ARCHAEOLOGICAL INSTITVTE OF AMERICA
FOVNDED 1879 · INCORPORATED 1906
MON V MEN TA PRIO RVM VI RVM

Chicago 1990

ISBN: 0-9609042-2-0

The views and opinions expressed are those of the writers and not necessarily those of the Archaeological Institute of America and its Chicago Society.

Copies of this publication are available through the Archaeological Institute of America, Kenmore Station, Box 1901, Boston, Massachusetts 02215, or its Chicago Society, 6215 North Neenah, Chicago, Illinois 60631.

TABLE OF CONTENTS

Centennial Symposium

THE ANCIENT EASTERN MEDITERRANEAN

PROGRAM

Robert D. Biggs	Welcome
Lanny Bell	The Epigraphic Survey and the Rescue of the Monuments of Ancient Egypt
George R. Hughes	The Epigraphic Survey—The Early Years
Robert J. Braidwood	Background on the Oriental Institute's Prehistoric Project
Karen L. Wilson	Oriental Institute Excavations at Khorsabad, Iraq
McGuire Gibson	Excavations at Nippur
Hans Güterbock	Hittites and the Dictionary
Douglas Esse	The Exploration of Megiddo
Edward F. Campbell	George Ernest Wright and the Shechem Expedition
Dennis E. Groh	Recent Indications of Hellenization at Ancient Sepphoris (Lower Galilee), Israel
Elizabeth R. Gebhard	Excavations at Isthmia and the Work of Oscar Broneer
Hector Williams	Kenchreai, Eastern Port of Corinth
James Russell	Kenchreai—A Personal View
Eric Pratt Hamp	Carl Darling Buck
Eleanor Guralnick	Chicago Museums and the Chicago Society
Jack Davis	Walking into the Future
Robert D. Biggs	Closing Remarks

SATURDAY MARCH 31, 1990

ACKNOWLEDGEMENTS

This volume is being published in conjunction with the symposium of the same name being held at the Oriental Institute March 31, 1990 to celebrate the centenary of the founding of the Chicago Society of the Archaeological Institute of America.

I wish to express thanks to all our AIA colleagues who agreed to make oral presentations at the symposium, most of whom have also contributed brief essays to this volume.

We are grateful to the Oriental Institute for allowing us to hold the symposium in Breasted Hall—named for James Henry Breasted, founder of the Oriental Institute, but also president of the Chicago Society of the AIA from 1920 to 1921, vice president from 1913 to 1918, and a member of its executive committee continuously from 1896 to 1935. While plans for the symposium were under discussion by the Executive Committee for some time, the main burden of organizing the symposium and handling the myriad details involved in editing and publishing this volume has been assumed by our former president, Eleanor Guralnick. Only someone who has been involved in such an undertaking can realize the time, effort, and devotion required to bring it to a successful conclusion. On behalf of the Chicago Society, I wish to express our full appreciation to her.

Several other people have also been very helpful. Gretel Braidwood, who has herself organized several symposia, was ready with practical advice. Karen Wilson, Curator of the Oriental Institute Museum, kindly gave permission to have a reception in the Egyptian Gallery of the Museum. Karen Bradley helped with registration details, and Thomas and Chris Urban agreed to handle setting up the coffee breaks and the reception following the symposium. Jean Fulton edited the text of the papers. Patricia Murray prepared the final camera-ready copy. Peter Kosiba and Alice Mulberry provided essential assistance in many ways.

To all who have helped to make our centennial celebration a memorable event, I express our deepest appreciation.

Robert D. Biggs
President, Chicago Society,
Archaeological Institute of America

PREFACE

In order to commemorate the 100th anniversary year of the founding of the Chicago Society of the Archaeological Institute of America, the symposium, "The Ancient Eastern Mediterranean," was convened and its papers published. Each of the speakers is or has been a member of the Chicago Society. Every one of the many individuals whose archaeological contributions are enumerated here are or were members. Readers will recognize the extraordinary importance and diversity of the projects undertaken by members of the Chicago Society and their impact on the science, art, and insights of archaeology.

The very large number of Chicago Society members who have been or are now professionals in archaeology have made it impossible for every project and every outstanding archaeologist to participate or to be recognized in this limited one-day program. Therefore, I would like to mention a few additional ongoing projects and their leaders who more than qualify for inclusion.

First among these is Helene J. Kantor, who has made extraordinary contributions to both the understanding of ancient art and to the illumination of the lives of early peoples of the Near East through her 20-year exploration and study of Choga Mish in western Iran. She has been a member of the Chicago Society for more than 40 years and has served it long and well as an officer and as a member of its executive committee.

Of equal stature, for his diverse contributions to knowledge through archaeological exploration, writing of history, and epigraphical and philological studies, is Hans Güterbock. The Hittite Dictionary, a project that he initiated and to which he contributed significantly, will remain a monument to his energy and intelligence, and will be the essential tool for generations of scholars yet to come. He, too, has been a member of the Chicago Society for some 40 years, serving as its president during the 1970s.

Another Chicagoan of seminal importance to the field of archaeology is zoologist Charles Reed. Recently, the Archaeological Institute of America honored him with the Pomerance Award for scientific contributions to archaeology for his pioneering studies of the domestication of animals from the analysis of faunal remains. He has worked with many other archaeologists in many countries as a consulting specialist.

Chicagoans' contributions to the exploration of the Greek site of Corinth have scarcely been alluded to in the text. David Moore Robinson, in 1903, initiated the Chicago relationship with these excavations, ongoing today. Two men, Robert L. Scranton (of the University of Chicago) and Carl Roebuck (of Northwestern

University) spent many seasons excavating at Corinth, and between them are responsible for the publication of several volumes reporting on those results. Mary Roebuck is now hard at work on another such volume. One of the papers does discuss Scranton's work and extraordinary finds at Kenchreai, while scarcely alluding to his pioneering underwater explorations of its sunken harbor installations.

Janet Johnson and Donald Whitcomb have done important explorations at Quseir, Thomas McClellan in Syria, and James Phillips and Lester Milligan of the Upper Paleolithic at Abu Noshra in the Sinai. James Packer has completed the first full study of the Basilica Ulpia, the largest public building of ancient Rome. Ira Mark completed his excavation and publication of the Sanctuary of Athena Nike on the Acropolis of Athens. Jack Davis is one of the pioneers who has demonstrated the usefulness of the comprehensive archaeological survey in providing insights into ancient cultures through consideration of regional settlement patterns and environments.

Among the earlier giants of archaeology whose work may have escaped mention in the papers, but who held membership in the Chicago Society and were leaders within it, are Henri Frankfort, Carl Kraeling, Pinhas Delougaz, Thomas George Allen, Charles Nims, and John Wilson, on the Near Eastern side. On the classical side, many who worked essentially with language and literature were most actively engaged in the leadership of the Chicago Society. Among these individuals were William Gardner Hale, Paul Shorey, Gordon Jennings Laing, Carl Darling Buck, Elmer Truesdale Merrill, Frank F. Abbott, and Gertrude Smith.

Other major institutions are related to the Chicago Society by means of the diverse interests and extraordinary energies of individuals who figure in the history of our city.

A few men of outstanding achievement in education, completely uninvolved in archaeology as a profession, served the Chicago Society. Harry Pratt Judson joined the society while he was still a professor of political sciences. He resigned the presidency of the Chicago Society some months after he became president of the University of Chicago. Frank Wakely Gunsaulas, the president of Armour Institute, the forerunner of the Illinois Institute of Technology, served simultaneously as president of the Chicago Society. Twice he presented lectures on ancient art to its members.

These men walked in the tradition of many of the founding and earliest members of the society, men who made significant contributions to the cultural life of the city of Chicago. In the brief introduction that follows, some of these men and their achievements will be mentioned.

Eleanor Guralnick

NOTES ABOUT THE AUTHORS

LANNY BELL, Ph.D.

Associate Professor of Egyptology in the Department of Near Eastern Languages and Civilizations at the University of Chicago. He conducted five field seasons (1967–74) of the University (of Chicago) Museum's Theban Tomb Project, while also serving as curatorial assistant (1965–77) in the Egyptian Section of the museum. As the field director of the Oriental Institute's Epigraphic Survey, his administrative responsibilities included organizing, implementing, and co-directing a major fundraising campaign which, after four years, has led to the establishment of two endowment funds dedicated to supporting the Epigraphic Survey. He has been teaching since 1965, began lecturing for the AIA in 1971, and has conducted many tours in Egypt since 1973. Among his publications is "Luxor Temple and the Cult of the Royal *Ka*," in *JNES* 44 (1985), the first comprehensive attempt to interpret the historical and theological significance of Luxor Temple within the ancient Egyptian cultural context. In recognition of his 12 years of service (1977–89) as field director of the Epigraphic Survey, he has recently been elected a corresponding member of the Deutsches Archäologisches Institut.

ROBERT J. BRAIDWOOD, Ph.D. and LINDA S. BRAIDWOOD, M.A.

Professor Emeritus of the Oriental Institute and the Department of Anthropology, University of Chicago. In 1929, he shifted from architecture (at the University of Michigan) to ancient history. In 1930–31, he worked with Michigan's Selucia-on-the-Tigris Expedition, then finished his M.A. in 1933. In that autumn, he joined the Institute's Syrian Expedition field staff, and first encountered reasonably early village-farming community materials. In 1937, Linda Braidwood became a field partner (as well as his wife). In 1947, the Oriental Institute's Prehistoric Project was founded, and three field seasons in Iraqi Kurdistan were followed by one season near Kermanshah in Iran, then by a succession of seasons as the Joint Prehistoric Project of Istanbul and Chicago universities, with Professor Dr. Halet Cambel as co-director. The project's focus of research attention has dealt with the formation of an effective village-farming community way of life in southwestern Asia. In 1971 Robert Braidwood was awarded the Gold Medal for Distinguished Archaeological Achievement by the Archaeological Institute of America. Linda Braidwood is Associate in Archaeology at the Oriental Institute.

EDWARD F. CAMPBELL, Ph.D.

Professor of Old Testament at McCormick Theological Seminary since 1958, he is a graduate of Yale University and McCormick Seminary. He completed his doctorate at Johns Hopkins University under W. F. Albright in 1959; his dissertation was published as a monograph, *The Chronology of the Amarna Letters*, in 1964. For many years the editor of *The Biblical Archaeologist* (published by the American Schools of Oriental Research), he assumed field direction of the Shechem project in 1966, and serves as the coordinator of its final publication. He is author of the commentary on Ruth in the Anchor Bible (1975), and divides his time between archaeological and biblical interpretation.

ELIZABETH R. GEBHARD, Ph.D.

Professor, Department of Classics, University of Illinois at Chicago. She has had visiting appointments at the University of Chicago (spring 1986–89), Wellesley College (spring 1985), and at the American School of Classical Studies in Athens (1983–84). She is currently director of the University of Chicago excavations at Isthmia, a position she has held since 1976. She has been associated with the Isthmia excavations since 1959, being actively involved in field work there 1959–62, 1967, and 1976 to the present. She has also excavated at Kenchreai (1963) and at Stobi in Yugoslavia (1970–81). Ancient theaters are her main professional interest. Her major publications include *The Theater at Isthmia* and the forthcoming *Theater at Stobi.* She has written on a variety of topics related to the Sanctuary of Poseidon at Isthmia, including articles on the Isthmian Games, metalworking, roof tiles, and wall decoration.

DENNIS E. GROH, Ph.D.

Associate Director of the University of South Florida excavations at Sepphoris, he is Professor of the History of Christianity at Garrett-Evangelical Theological Seminary and an Advisory Member of the Graduate Faculty of Northwestern University. Groh is Vice President of the Chicago Society of the AIA. In addition to Sepphoris, he has excavated at Caesarea Maritima, Merion, Gush Halav, and en-Nabratein. He currently also serves as archaeological consultant to the Tell Nitzana excavations of Ben-Gurion University of the Negev, having held the Humphrey Fellowship of that university's Humphrey Institute for Social Ecology. He is a past president of the North American Patristic Society and a former annual professor of the W. F. Albright Institute of Archaeological Research in Jerusalem.

ELEANOR GURALNICK, Ph.D.

An unaffiliated research scholar who earned her Ph.D. from the University of Chicago. Her educational background includes studies in both classical and Near Eastern archaeology and art. Her main published works on Greek art document some of the connections between the art of early Greece and those of Egypt and the Near East. She was the first to demonstrate that computer-executed statistical methods applied to works of art can illuminate long-standing and controversial problems. Her research has been supported by grants from the National Endowment for the Humanities, the American Philosophical Society, and the German Academic Exchange Service. She has been a member of the executive committee of the Chicago Society since 1971, serving as president (1982–86), vice president (1978–82), and as secretary (1972–78). She is a member of the symposium committee and has served on the membership committee of the Archaeological Institute of America. Presently, she is keeper of the archive for the Chicago Society.

ERIC PRATT HAMP, Ph.D.

Robert Maynard Hutchins Distinguished Service Professor for Linguistics, Psychology, Slavic Languages and Linguistics, Committee on the Ancient Mediterranean World; Director of the Center for Balkan and Slavic Studies at the University of Chicago. He is a past president of the Linguistic Society of America; editor of *Notes and Review* and the *International Journal of American Linguistics*, and co-editor of the *Native American Texts Series*. He is also the linguistic consultant and analyst for the Braille Reading and Language Program of the American Printing House for the Blind in Louisville, Kentucky. He has done a major study of dialectology, resulting in his *Atlas Linguarum Europae, Scottish Gaelic Dialect Atlas*. His field work includes the Linguistic Survey of Scotland (Edinburgh), of the Albanian enclaves of Greece, of Yugoslavia, Bulgaria, and Italy; Resian dialect (Friuli), Romanian, and of the Ojibwa, Algonquian, and Quileute Native American languages.

GEORGE R. HUGHES, Ph.D.

Oriental Institute Professor Emeritus of Egyptology, University of Chicago. A member of the Epigraphic Survey at Luxor, Egypt (1946–64), he was its director 1949–63. He was director of the Epigraphic Survey 1949–63, and participated in the Nubian Expedition of the Oriental Institute and was director of it at Serra East in the Sudan. He taught in Chicago (1964–77) and served as director of the Oriental Institute 1968–72. The texts, grammar, and lexicography of Demotic Egyptian have been his major areas of research and publications; he now serves as consultant for the Chicago Demotic Dictionary Project. His many honors include his election to the Institut d'Égypte and the Deutsches Archäologisches Institut.

HECTOR WILLIAMS, Ph.D.

Associate Professor in Department of Classics at the University of British Columbia (UBC) in Vancouver. He began his archaeological field work at the University of Chicago's Kenchreai project in 1968 and subsequently worked at American School of Classical Studies in Athens excavations at Corinth and Samothrace. From 1971 to 1985 he was assistant director and photographer at UBC's excavations of Roman Anemurium in southern Turkey, as well as continuing as research associate at Kenchreai whose Greek and Roman lamps he published in 1981. Since 1980 he has also been associated with the University of Pennsylvania's excavations at Gordion. From 1981 to 1984 he was director of the new Canadian Archaeological Institute at Athens and set up its facilities and programs for a consortium of 40 Canadian universities and government agencies. Since 1982 he has directed its projects at Stymphalos and Mytilene in Greece. His other major field of interest is maritime archaeology; he helped set up the Underwater Archaeological Society of British Columbia. His archaeological photography has appeared in 15 journals, including covers of *Archaeology* and *Antike Welt.*

KAREN L. WILSON, Ph.D.

Curator of the Oriental Institute Museum at the University of Chicago. She was the director of the Institute of Fine Arts Expedition to Tell Genj, Iraq (1977–78) and the Institute of Fine Arts Mendes Expedition, Egypt (1979–81). Publications include *Mendes, Preliminary Report on the 1979 and 1980 Seasons* (Cities of the Delta, II) and "Nippur: The Definition of a Mesopotamian Jamdat Nasr Assemblage," in U. Finkbeiner and W. Röllig (eds.), *Gamdat Nasr Period or Regional Style?*

INTRODUCTION—THE CHICAGO SOCIETY

Eleanor Guralnick

On November 4, 1889 a group of cultural leaders of Chicago were brought together at the invitation of Mr. and Mrs. Franklin MacVeagh to learn of the proposal of the Greek government to offer the concession to excavate the ruins of the ancient Sanctuary of Apollo at Delphi to an American association, provided that a guarantee fund sufficient to cover the cost of the site were raised in a reasonably brief length of time. Those who wished to establish a Chicago Society of the Archaeological Institute of America then adjourned to the home of Mr. and Mrs. Charles L. Hutchinson where it was resolved to establish such a society. Officers and an executive committee were elected, and a set of rules was adopted.

The first annual business meeting was held on December 20, 1889 and the first general lecture meeting was held on February 21, 1890 at the home of Marshall Field, 1905 Prairie Avenue.

From the very beginning the membership included both leaders in the cultural life of the city and faculty at its institutions of higher education. Among the founders were such men as Marshall Field (founder of the Field Museum of Natural History), Charles L. Hutchinson (president of the Art Institute), Edward Everett Ayer (a director of the Art Institute, Chairman of the Board of Trustees of the Field Museum, and a trustee of the University of Chicago), Franklin MacVeagh (later Secretary of the Treasury of the United States), Martin A. Ryerson (who was Chairman of the Board of Trustees of the University of Chicago, established the Martin A. Ryerson Library at the Art Institute and scholarships for the study of archaeology at the University of Chicago), Norman Williams (first president of the Crerar Library), A. A. Sprague (second president of the Crerar Library), Eliphalet

Blatchford (a founder and first president of Newberry Library), Dr. William F. Poole (head of the Newberry Library), A. C. Bartlett (president of the Chicago Board of Education), Bryan Lathrop (a founder and president of the Chicago Orchestral Association), Frank G. Logan (patron of the Chicago Civic Opera), and Dr. Emil G. Hirsch (reform rabbi of Sinai Temple, grandfather of Edward Levi who became president of the University of Chicago). Others who joined during the early years included Mr. and Mrs. Potter Palmer, Cyrus McCormick, Lorado Taft (sculptor), John J. Glessner (whose home, the scene of several early meetings, is now the home of the Chicago Architecture Foundation), John G. Shedd (founder of the Shedd Aquarium), Clarence Buckingham (to whom the Buckingham Fountain is dedicated), Daniel Burnham (who designed and built Chicago's lakefront), and Julius Rosenwald (founder of the Museum of Science and Industry).

These people did not merely join. They all served on the Executive Committee and as officers of the society. Almost all served the society throughout the rest of their lives. Many, together with their spouses, children, grandchildren, great-grandchildren, and family connections retained membership through most of the century.

In the earliest years classical archaeologists Alfred Emerson and Frank B. Tarbell were interested in building Chicago's museum collections and in studying museum artifacts. Following the establishment of the University of Chicago in 1892, faculty in the Classics Department joined in support of archaeology, with many classicists filling offices. These people included such luminaries as William G. Hale, Gordon Laing, Elmer T. Merrill, Carl H. Beeson, Edward Capps, Gertrude Smith, Frank F. Abbott, Paul Shorey, and Oscar Broneer, among others. As the University of Chicago matured, classical archaeologists such as Peter Von Blanckenhagen, Franklin Plotinus Johnson, and Robert L. Scranton became members of the Art Department, in some cases holding multiple departmental appointments. These individuals carried major responsibilities for the society throughout its 100-year history.

In 1896 James H. Breasted joined the executive committee and for the next 39 years he was continuously involved in the leadership of the Chicago Society, making an important contribution to the diversity of the programs. The strength of the society grew as it included ever more members who were archaeologists working in the Near East. John Wilson carried on this tradition of leadership for the next 40 years. Many others from the Oriental Institute served the Chicago Society, including Edward Chiera, Carl H. Kraeling, Thomas George Allen, Ignace I. Gelb, Pinhas Delougaz, Henri Frankfort, Keith Seele, Robert and Linda Braidwood, Gustavus F. Swift, Hans Güterbock, Helene Kantor, and Robert Biggs. In recent years the strong support of Janet H. Johnson has been invaluable to the society. Today many of the excavators, both faculty and students, are members of the Chicago Society. Many museum volunteers are not only members but have provided many valuable services for which we thank them.

Lest we forget, faculty from several Chicago-area universities and colleges have been actively involved in leadership positions with the Chicago Society. From the time of the founding of Northwestern University, many of its classics faculty have also been actively involved in Chicago Society leadership. Roy C. Flickinger, Dean of the Liberal Arts, and Ernest Highbarger were two who together offered nearly 40 years of devoted service. Carl Roebuck and James Packer have successively filled this role during the more recent 40 years.

Both the McCormick and Garrett Theological seminaries have long had commitments to archaeology and the Chicago Society. Cyrus H. McCormick, founder of the seminary that bears the McCormick name, was only the first of a long line of family members and descendants to support the Chicago Society through membership. Professor Otis Beeson served the society as its secretary for many years. A president of the Garrett-Evangelical Theological Seminary was a long-time member of the executive committee of the society. Today, Edward Campbell and Dennis Groh continue this tradition of excellent archaeological work together with Edgar Krenz of the Lutheran School of Theology.

In the past few decades the University of Illinois has developed a very active program in archaeology. Elizabeth Gebhard, Jack Davis, Charles Reed, James Phillips, and Lester Milligan are leading the way to a new archaeology for the 21st century.

Faculty of the Classics Department of Loyola University of Chicago have been getting ever more deeply involved in excavation. Raymond V. Schoder, S.J., initiated this trend when he excavated an early Greek settlement in Marseilles, France. Edward Kase continued with his major investigation of Bronze Age road systems in Northern Greece. Robert Sutton spent many seasons working on the American School-sponsored excavations and surveys centered about Nemea, Greece. In recent years anthropologist Francis X. Grollig, S.J., has been excavating in the Americas and taking an active role in the Chicago Society.

Chicago Society founding father, Charles A. Hutchinson, brought together in his home a group of leading citizens, for the express purpose of founding a Chicago Society of the Archaeological Institute of America. He became first president of the society, serving in this capacity for six years, as vice president for eight years, and as a member of the executive committee for 36 years until his death. He became the Chicago Society's first life member in 1889. Through all the years he served simultaneously as president of the Art Institute of Chicago. He and the director of the museum, William M. R. French (also a Chicago Society member) assembled the core of the present Classical Collection of that museum.

Edward Everett Ayer was one of the very first to join the newly formed AIA, serving as president for eight years, vice president for 18 and as member of the executive committee for 30. He was instrumental in establishing the ancient collections of the Field Museum of Natural History.

Martin A. Ryerson, a founding and life member of the Chicago Society purchased the Tomb of Unis Ankh for the Field Museum. A philanthropist, he generously gave many objects of ancient art to the Art Institute and contributed his private library of books on art and archaeology to establish the Martin A. Ryerson Library at that museum. His gifts to the University of Chicago included many books on classical art and archaeology, which are now in the Regenstein Library Special Collections. And, many students at the University of Chicago have benefited from his generous gift to establish scholarships and fellowships for study, travel, and research in classical archaeology. This generous benefactor to generations of students at the University of Chicago served on the Chicago Society's executive committee for 35 years. For 30 of those years (1892–1922) he was Chairman of the Board of Trustees of the University of Chicago.

The very first secretary of the Chicago Society was Alfred Emerson. As a professor at Lake Forest University (now Lake Forest College), he led that institution to become a founding member of the Chicago Society. After his appointment to be Professor of Archaeology at the University of Chicago, he became also honorary curator of the Classical Collection of the Art Institute. Subsequently, the curatorial position became his primary responsibility. At his death in 1944 he had been a member of the Chicago Society for 55 years and was the last surviving founding member.

In 1892 Frank Bigelow Tarbell became secretary of the Chicago Society, serving as president for 10 years and on the executive committee a total of 30 years. Tarbell, a scholar of classical art, was responsible for transforming the University's Department of Archaeology into the Department of Art.

William Gardner Hale (president of the Chicago Society 1896–1899 and University of Chicago's Classics Department Chairman) contributed to the University's classical museum the collection of prehistoric potsherds that he had acquired from Heinrich Schliemann. Relatively recently the collection of Carl Darling Buck was presented to the Smart Gallery by his daughter-in-law. Buck was a Chicago Society executive committee member, and a Professor of Indo-European Linguistics at the University of Chicago for over 40 years. He also spent some years of his youth at the American School of Classical Studies in Athens and in 1888 had excavated for one season at Ikaria, Greece.

A non-archaeological tradition governed the professional work of many of those who worked most tirelessly for the Chicago Society of the Archaeological Institute of America. Most of these individuals were professors in the Classics Department of the University of Chicago, whose professional interests ranged from classical language and literature to philosophy, religion, politics, and history.

Gordon Jennings Laing wrote books on such varied topics as *Masterpieces of Latin Literature, Selections from Ovid, The Genitive of Value in Latin ...*, and with Paul Shorey the second revised edition of Shorey's *Odes and Epodes of Horace*. The closest he ever came to digging archaeology was in his written review of *The Topography and Monuments of Ancient Rome*. Paul Shorey, a long-time member of the Chicago Society, was chiefly interested in Latin literature and Greek philosophy and history. He wrote studies of the works of Aristotle, Plato, Thucydides, and, of course, Horace and of still others. William Gardner Hale prepared his *Latin Grammar for Schools and Colleges* with Carl Darling Buck. He produced dozens of papers on points of Latin and Greek grammar. Elmer Truesdale Merrill focused some of his professional attention to the works of Pliny. Charles Henry Beeson was mainly interested in Latin philology and produced *A New Second Latin Book*. Frank F. Abbott published critical analyses of *The Letters of Cicero, A History and Description of Roman Political Institutions, Handbook for the Study of Roman History* and *A Short History of Rome*. Gertrude Smith was concerned with such subjects as the "Athenian Casualty Lists" published in *Classical Philology*. Carl Darling Buck was a giant in the study of Greek and Latin languages from the structural and linguistic point of view and was a progenitor of the present Department of Linguistics at the University of Chicago.

Yet, each of the above individuals was a member of the executive committee of the Chicago Society for all or most of his or her professional life. Laing, Merrill, Beeson, and Smith each did yeomanly work as secretary for nearly 20 years on average.

Several Chicago Society members sustained very long-term involvements with the excavations at Corinth sponsored by the American School of Classical Studies. Publication of this material offered them scope for both art historical and architectural studies. This association was initiated by David Moore Robinson, a graduate student in classical archaeology when he led both the Chicago Society and the excavation of ancient Corinth in 1904. In 1905 he published a paper on "The Corinth Terra Cotta Finds." He went on to do splendid work at Corinth, Olynthus and elsewhere in Greece. A couple of decades later Franklin Plotinus Johnson wrote the volume on *Sculpture 1896–1923, Corinth*, Vol. IX. Years later two other members of the Chicago Society excavated at Corinth for many seasons resulting in contributions to architectural history. Robert L. Scranton, *Architecture*, Vol. I, pt. 2, *Monuments in the Lower Agora and North of the Archaic Temple*, Vol. I, pt. 3 and *Medieval Architecture in the Central Area of Corinth*, Vol. XVI, and Carl Roebuck, *The Asklepieion and Lerna*, Vol. XIV. Carl and Mary Roebuck (now retired from Northwestern University, Department of Classics) are presently in Greece where Mary is engaged in preparing an additional volume, *The Architectural Terra Cottas*, for publication. Scranton and Roebuck are just a couple of the digging classical archaeologists of the Chicago Society. Elizabeth Gebhard and Hector Williams will tell us much more about these men and of other major figures of the Chicago Society who engaged in major excavations of the classical world.

REFERENCES

Archive
1889–1990 Archive of the Chicago Society, Archaeological Institute of America.

Andreas, A. T.
1886 *History of Chicago*. Chicago.

Drury, J.
1941 *Old Chicago Houses*. Chicago.

Gilbert, P. and C. L. Bryson
1929 *Chicago and Its Makers*. Chicago.

Pierce, B. L.
1957 *A History of Chicago*. New York.

THE EPIGRAPHIC SURVEY AND THE RESCUE OF THE MONUMENTS OF ANCIENT EGYPT

Lanny Bell

JAMES Henry Breasted "was effectively the founder of American Egyptology" (Baines and Málek 1980, 29). Upon the awarding of his doctorate from Berlin University in 1894, he was appointed (at the age of 29) to the first chair of Egyptology in America, newly established at the fledgling University of Chicago (UC), then itself not yet three years old. After their first cruise up the Nile on their honeymoon, the Breasteds took up residence in Chicago in 1895. By 1898, he was a member of the executive committee of the Chicago Society of the AIA, becoming its vice president by 1913, and serving as its president in 1920–21. In 1919 he founded the Oriental Institute at the University of Chicago, remaining its director until his death in 1935.

By his personal dedication and charisma, Breasted was able to attract a circle of very talented, conscientious, and forward-looking colleagues to his cause, as well as gaining and keeping the support of enthusiastic and loyal financial backers, a felicitous combination that ensured his success in the realization of his great vision. Nearly singlehandedly he determined the future course of Egyptology at the University of Chicago, down to this day. Besides laying the foundations for the Oriental Institute Museum's Egyptian collection and the Demotic Dictionary Project, carrying out his own photographic expedition to Nubia, and organizing the Epigraphic Survey and her sister Architectural Survey (which completed the excavations of Medinet Habu in 1927–33), he instituted the Sakkarah Expedition, the Coffin Texts Project, and the joint epigraphic expedition of the British Egypt Exploration Society and the Oriental Institute to the Temple of Sety I at Abydos.

Breasted was succeeded in the directorship of the Oriental Institute (OI) by John Wilson, who eventually became my professor at the University of Chicago.

Wilson immediately joined the executive committee of the Chicago AIA (in which capacity he served for 30 years), becoming society president in 1939–41. A staff member of the Epigraphic Survey (1926–31) and its field director in 1958–59, Wilson also acted as executive secretary for the United States National Committee for the Preservation of the Nubian Monuments during he UNESCO International Campaign for the Safeguard of the Monuments of Nubia, from 1959 to 1971 raising the equivalent of more than $16 million as the U.S.A.'s contribution to this great effort. At the same time, the Oriental Institute Nubian Expedition, under the general directorship of UC professor and AIA member, Keith Seele, conducted several excavations near the Egyptian-Sudanese frontier (under continuing publication by OI Research Associate and AIA member Bruce Williams), while the energies of the Epigraphic Survey, then with George Hughes as field director, were turned to recording the temple of Ramesses II at Beit el-Wali. To round out this very brief summary of Oriental Institute Egyptological activities in which AIA members have played major roles, mention should be made of the recent excavations of UC Professor Janet H. Johnson and her husband, OI Research Associate Donald Whitcomb, at the Roman and Islamic port of Quseir (1977–82) on the Red Sea coast and in the mound of Medieval Luxor city (1985–86) just to the north of Luxor Temple.

But let us now focus our attention on the Epigraphic Survey, the longest-running American archaeological mission operating in Egypt, and one of the longest-standing major research commitments of the Oriental Institute. Established in Egypt in 1924, two years after the discovery of the Tomb of Tutankhamun, and based at Chicago House in Luxor, this expedition was organized **exclusively** to document the scenes and inscriptions on the walls of the endangered and rapidly decaying Pharaonic monuments of the Theban area, arguably the largest concentration of ancient buildings still standing anywhere in the world. The word "epigraphic" refers to its study and recording of monumental decoration, mostly inscribed on stone or plaster (as opposed to papyrology, for instance); and "survey" refers to its pioneer mapping of the carved and painted reliefs covering nearly every surface of the temples of the Theban area (Nelson 1941). The world-renowned "Chicago House method" of epigraphy, developed in the formative years of the project, employs an ingenious combination of photographs and inked facsimile line-drawings, every one produced by a team of skilled specialists, working together and checking each other's results, to achieve the detailed accuracy and completeness for which the survey is justly famous. The staff is on site in Luxor for six months every year, so that all checking of drawings can be done directly at the walls.

In the past 66 years, Chicago House has become a major international center for research into all aspects of the civilization of ancient Egypt. Its resources include a photo archive of 15,000 large-format (8"×10" and 5"×7") negatives and some 20,000 prints, which provides the most extensive photographic coverage of Theban temples and tombs available in one place anywhere in the world. The comprehensive Egyptological library of 15,500 volumes is one of the best in the world, is rivaled in size and scope in Egypt only by the library of the Cairo Museum, and is the only library of Egyptology within Egypt located south of Cairo. Use of these and other facilities has been traditionally extended as a professional courtesy to scholars of all nationalities.

The Epigraphic Survey remains a purely private research institution (Chicago House being the headquarters of the University of Chicago in Egypt), working under annual contract with the Egyptian Antiquities Organization. The survey was the creation of James Henry Breasted, who, during his first trip up the Nile with his new bride in 1894–95, had been appalled as he became aware of the enormous amount of damage the standing monuments of Egypt had suffered since the days that the earliest recording missions (Napoleon's expedition of 1798–1801, Champollion and Rosellini in 1828–29, and Lepsius in 1842–45) had worked on them. He declared that there should be a moratorium on further exploration and excavation, and that the real priority should be complete and accurate publication of all the monuments already known.

The threat to the monuments was not new in Breasted's time, it was not discovered by him, nor was it a secret known only to him. The fragile ecology of many formerly half-buried temples had been destabilized as they were rapidly exposed one after another through excavations conducted in the middle of the 19th century. Some structures apparently perceived as of little historical significance or artistic merit were dismantled merely to quickly obtain building materials. The pattern was clear, and the response within Egypt was swift. The year 1857, in fact, saw the founding of the Egyptian Antiquities Organization (then known as the Service des Antiquités de l'Egypte) by August Mariette.

> Mariette's three greatest achievements were, the creation of the first National Antiquities Service, the formation of the first National Museum in the Near East ..., and the developing of a firstly Egyptian then world-wide conscience about the destruction, expropriation, and proper care and conservation of antiquities; backed by de Lesseps [the "father" of the Suez Canal] he made a successful plea to Said Pasha for an organization to deal with the standing Egyptian monuments which were being rapidly destroyed ... (Dawson and Uphill 1972, 195).

Nevertheless, the situation continued to deteriorate down to Breasted's day, and the danger is even more serious today.

Apart from "natural" erosion (caused by wind, rain, sun, and the actions of animals) and normal wear and tear associated with tourism, the greatest threat to the monuments today is posed by their confrontation with the relentless forces intruding upon them from the modern world, represented by the pressures of industrialization, overpopulation, urban growth, and the need for agricultural development. Twentieth-century Egypt simply **must** farm and build beyond the narrow confines of ancient Egypt, encroaching on sites that were once safely situated in forbidding or uninhabitable desert zones. The main danger facing the monuments on or immediately adjacent to the old flood plain of the Nile is waste-water disposal and the infiltration of dissolved water-borne salts drawn up into the ancient stones by capillary action, recrystallizing and growing in and on them, disintegrating the very fabric of the stone, undermining foundations and obscuring and finally destroying decorated surfaces. This condition has worsened significantly in the past 20 years as new agricultural patterns associated with the construction of the Aswan High Dam have prevailed—the end of the annual inundation, the overall raising of the normal level of the ground water (even in years when the Nile itself has been incredibly low), the increase in humidity resulting from the expansion of the open canal irrigation system, and the use of chemical fertilizers—all encouraging the movement of water and salts.

Modern Egypt houses the most impressive collection of monumental ancient remains of any nation on earth, and tourism plays a crucial role in Egypt's economy. In many respects, Egypt **is** a vast outdoor museum, and museums are to be visited. Tourism, in fact, enhances the value of the monuments, as well as enriching the significance of our scholarly and scientific efforts on their behalf. But tourism is also part of the problem. The ancient tombs and temples were sacred places in antiquity, and access to them was strictly regulated. Although many distinguished Greco-Roman and later visitors were attracted to them, they have never before been subjected to such regular and heavy traffic as now, Until the advent of cheap international airfare, who could have envisioned an annual influx of more than one million tourists coming specifically to visit the antiquities of Egypt? Thousands of people every day tramping on floors, kicking up dust, bumping against or thoughtlessly touching walls, breathing, coughing, and perspiring in closed, cramped, unair-conditioned spaces—this is what the monuments are up against. The difficulty for any archaeologist or museum curator is finding the best way to display an artifact, even an artifact as large as a temple, that will balance its safeguard against access for tourism. In the end, a major part of the solution may lie simply in the direction of educating the tourist public to the needs of the monuments.

Dr. Ahmed Qadry, former president of the Egyptian Antiquities Organization (EAO), reported at the Fourth International Congress of Egyptology (held in Munich in the late summer of 1985) that the EAO was currently spending £E 15 million annually (revenue collected from the fees visitors pay to enter antiquities sites) on conservation and restoration throughout Egypt on Pharaonic, Coptic, and Islamic monuments. Many sites have recently been restored and opened; some over-visited monuments are periodically closed for maintenance or restoration, or simply to prolong their existence; the number of persons permitted to enter small tombs at one time is limited; flash photography inside the tombs is forbidden; roads and parking lots have been relocated to prevent vibrations caused by the traffic of heavy motor vehicles, particularly buses, from damaging delicate walls; and toilets have been installed at major sites.

In spite of all this, Egypt was rocked two years ago when a chunk of stone crashed down unexpectedly from the shoulder of the Great Sphinx at Giza. Yet the tide of destruction is just cresting; and by the end of the next century, many more monuments, including some of the greatest of those still standing, will no longer exist as "intact" structures. This concern is not Egypt's alone: the conservation of historic sites is truly an international priority. For example, visitors are now prevented from entering the great circle at Stonehenge, the Parthenon is off limits to tourists on the Acropolis in Athens, and the painted caves in France, Spain, and India have been closed. A recent article decries the disintegration of the imperial monuments of the Roman capital itself and calls for a world effort to document and consolidate them (Nylander 1988). But physical preservation is extremely expensive: the "salvage" of Abu Simbel cost $39 million in 1965 (perhaps equivalent to some $300 million today), with ongoing maintenance still required.

Contrary to the situation that existed when Breasted started the Epigraphic Survey, artifacts may no longer be regarded as safely neglected when they are left untouched in the earth. Now they are increasingly threatened wherever they may lie buried, and one cannot continue to advocate the cessation of all excavation. Nevertheless, archaeology must not be thought of merely as excavation; although the survey does no excavation, its work is really a form of salvage archaeology. Sadly, we are not in a position to guarantee the long-term physical survival of the monuments on which we work; but, thanks to Breasted's foresight, we are able to preserve them through photography and the production and publication of precise facsimile drawings that are as complete and accurate as humanly possible. "The years will only enhance the importance of that work, for whereas pure scholarship dates rapidly, faithful copies grow in value according as destruction exacts its relentless toll" (Gardiner 1942, 60). And if our primary source material is inadequate or inaccurate in the first place, the conclusions we try to draw from the raw data must always be suspect at the very best.

Sixteen documentary volumes by the Epigraphic Survey have already appeared in print: *Medinet Habu* I–VIII, *Reliefs and Inscriptions at Karnak* I–IV, *Khonsu* I–II, *Kheruef*, and *Beit el-Wali*. A few comments from some of the most recent reviews and other references to the work of the Epigraphic Survey may be quoted here to help in assessing and evaluating its impact on the field of Egyptology as a whole.

> The quality of the plates, the result of the well-known "Chicago method," is of a level by which other archaeological publications may be judged (Peck 1980, 109).

> Es dürfte kaum nötig sein, zu betonen, daß die Tafeln mit den Zeichnungen der Darstellungen und Inschriften dem bekannt hohen Standard der 'Epigraphic Survey' entsprechen und keine Wünsche offen lassen (Graefe 1982, 63).

Like its predecessors, the book is a model of its kind (Rusmann 1984, 103).

Toute publication de la prestigieuse série de l'OIC est en soi un événement.... En bref, voilà une publication épigraphique modèle (Vernus 1984, 163–4).

La technique employée par l'équipe du Chicago House de Louqsor approche la perfection (Traunecker and Golvin 1984, 207, caption to Fig. 191).

From the point of view of accuracy, draughtsmanship, and neatness of presentation these admirable facsimiles leave nothing to be desired; no higher praise may be sung of them than to say that they are up to the loftiest long-established standards of The Epigraphic Survey. ... as a pictorial record of an ancient monument, it is impeccable and definitive and will not fail to command the admiration and gratitude of all Egyptologists now and for a long time to come (Caminos 1985, 199–200).

The author is well aware of the fact that a free-hand copy cannot be regarded as equal to a facsimile in its accuracy. Indeed, the facsimile method was developed to unrivalled perfection by the Oriental Institute in the publication of the Ramesside temples in Thebes (Kákosy 1985, 316).

Now, having before our eyes the best specimens of palaeography, such as those presented by Nina and Norman de Garis Davies, copyists of the Oriental Institute of the University of Chicago, and H. G. Fischer, we cannot be satisfied with the former level of text copying and of knowledge of hieroglyphic palaeography (Bogoslovsky 1985, 88).

One of the most important and urgent services that any person, group or institution can render to Egyptology today is the precise recording and accurate publication of the standing monuments of Egypt, principally her temples, tombs and rock texts and art. As ecological and demographic conditions change—almost always for the worse, so far as ancient remains are concerned—the surviving documents of the past come under ever-increasing threats to their very existence.

Hence it is with immense pleasure that one greets the publication of a further epigraphic volume by the team of the Chicago Oriental

> Institute, on this occasion editing the famous war-scenes of Sethos I at Karnak.
>
> Initially, long ago, this reviewer had privately wondered whether it was a wise use of resources to expend the 'Chicago' treatment upon this wall—so well known to scholars, and tolerably available in the plates of Wreszinski and sundry other sources. However, this virtually definitive publication has produced results which fully justify in every way the care and time devoted to this particular project. ...
>
> In short, one cannot do other than reiterate the capital importance and splendid quality of this latest Chicago epigraphic production. If only all the war-reliefs (and for that matter, all the temples!) were so fortunate in their choice of epigraphers! (Kitchen 1988).

The achievement of success in epigraphy is certainly not a simple mechanical process, and so-called "copying" is not as easy as you might think; it may be neither rushed nor pursued idly. The eyes and hands must be constantly at work, with the mind alert at all times; persistence and absolute concentration are required. If you are examining a wall that could easily be damaged or that might not exist at all in a relatively short time, it is necessary to be as thorough as possible, while trying to anticipate questions that may arise later and issues that might prove to be important in the future. Epigraphy is like detective work, like puzzle-solving; documentation and interpretation must always proceed hand-in-hand. All too often you see only what you expect to see, but every relief or painting actually contains much more information than appears at first glance. To fully understand and record all the available evidence that may be obscured in an altered or particularly broken or damaged section of wall, it is necessary to be familiar with the parallels so you can anticipate what **ought** to be there; you must learn to ask not only **what** is represented, but even what is **not** represented. Once you have made your proposal, you must reexamine the actual traces, testing and modifying your hypothesis accordingly. The Epigraphic Survey's activities are not limited to copying only inscriptions; it also draws the scenes in which these texts are embedded and of which they form an integral part. Each final production is a faithful rendering of an ancient Egyptian work of art in the broadest sense (including the hieroglyphic script).

Let me leave you with two facts that I continue to find astonishing: namely, that most of the more than 2,000 fabulous objects discovered in the tomb of Tutankhamun have not yet been adequately published; you must visit the Cairo Museum to examine them. The same is true of the breathtaking temple of Ramesses II at Abu Simbel, which more than half a million tourists visit each year since it was saved from the rising flood waters behind the Aswan High Dam; you must travel with them nearly to the Sudanese frontier (and take your binoculars) if you wish to study it thoroughly. And these are by no means isolated examples of the lack of reliable and complete documentation for "well-known" monuments. But whereas we may rest assured that the artifacts preserved in the Cairo Museum are relatively safe for tomorrow, what about the monuments that remain in situ? We may well be the last generation of scholars to have the opportunity to record many of the monuments that are taken for granted today; future generations will have to depend on our documentation. The Epigraphic Survey is proud of the role it has played in the international effort to preserve Egypt's ancient heritage; but it cannot rest upon its laurels as long as there are monuments still in need of recording, as long as there is money to pay the bills, and as long as the Egyptian people continue to welcome its assistance. This brief presentation can perhaps help you better appreciate why, after the 168 years since the decipherment of the hieroglyphs by Champollion in 1822, everything is not yet known about all the ancient Egyptian monuments, and why the work of Chicago House is always so rewarding.

REFERENCES

Baines, J. and J. Málek

1980 *Atlas of Ancient Egypt.* Oxford.

Bell, L.

1986 L'Epigraphic Survey, in *Histoire et Archéologie: Les Dossiers.* Dijon. 101: 92–4.

1987 The Epigraphic Survey: The Philosophy of Egyptian Epigraphy after Sixty Years' Practical Experience, in J. Assmann, G. Burkard, and V. Davies, *Problems and Priorities in Egyptian Archaeology.* London and New York, 43–55 and plates 1–6.

Bell, L., W. Murnane, and B. Fishman

1982a The Epigraphic Survey (Chicago House), *NARCE* 118: 3–23.

1982b The Epigraphic Survey (Chicago House). Part 2: The Institute Function of Chicago House (with Special Reference to the 1980–81 Field Season), *NARCE* 119: 5–13.

Bogoslovsky, E. S.

1985 Review of M. L. Bierbrier, *Hieroglyphic Texts from Egyptian Stelae,* 10 (London, 1982), *BibO* 42: 87–91.

Breasted, J. H.

1930 Foreword, in *Medinet Habu* I. Chicago, ix–xi.

1933 The Epigraphic Expedition, in *The Oriental Institute.* Chicago, 187–223.

Caminos, R. A.
1976 The Recording of Inscriptions and Scenes in Tombs and Temples, in R. A. Caminos and H. G. Fischer, *Ancient Egyptian Epigraphy and Paleography*. New York, 3–25.
1985 Review of *The Tomb of Kheruef*, Chicago, 1980, *JEA* 71: 197–200.

Dawson, W. R. and E. P. Uphill
1972 *Who Was Who in Egyptology*. 2nd ed. London.

Gardiner, A. H.
1942 Norman De Garis Davies. *JEA* 28: 59–60.

Graefe, E.
1982 Review of *The Tomb of Kheruef*, Chicago, 1980, *BibO* 39: 63–67.

Hughes, G. R.
1952 Recording Egypt's Ancient Documents, *Archaeology* 5: 201–4.

Kákosy, L.
1985 Review of C. M. Zivie, *Le Temple de Deir Chelouit* I (Cairo, 1982), *BibO* 42: 315–17.

Kitchen, K. A.
1988 Review of *The Battle Reliefs of King Sety* I, Chicago, 1986, *BibO* 45: 319–22.

Nelson, H. H.
1941 *Key Plans Showing Locations of Theban Temple Decorations*, Chicago.

Nims, C. F.
1973 The Publication of Ramesside Temples in Thebes by the Oriental Institute, in *Textes et languages de l'Egypte pharaonique* II. Cairo, 89–94.

Nylander, C.
1988 S.O.S. for Ancient Monuments, *Archaeology* 41.4: 54ff.

Peck, W. H.
1980 Review of *The Tomb of Kheruef*, Chicago, 1980, *JARCE* 17: 107–9.

Russmann, E. R.
1984 Review of *The Temple of Khonsu* I, Chicago, 1979, *Serapis* 7 (1981–82): 103–6.

Traunecker, C.
1987 Les Techniques d'épigraphie de terrain: Principes et pratique, in J. Assmann, G. Burkard, and V. Davies, *Problems and Priorities in Egyptian Archaeology*. London and New York, 261–98 and plates 28–31.

Traunecker, C. and J.-C. Golvin
1984 *Karnak: Résurrection d'un site*. Paris.

Vernus, P.
1984 Review of *The Temple of Khonsu* I, Chicago, 1979, *JEA* 70: 163–5.

THE EPIGRAPHIC SURVEY—THE EARLY YEARS

George R. Hughes

INASMUCH as James H. Breasted, who had founded the Oriental Institute at the University of Chicago, established "The Epigraphic and Architectural Survey" at Luxor (ancient Thebes) in Upper Egypt in 1924, my wife, Maurine, and I did not see "Chicago House" until the early autumn of 1946; I can scarcely speak from first-hand knowledge of the "early" years of the expedition.

To be sure, Harold H. Nelson, who had taken his doctorate under Breasted and had been lured to Luxor by Breasted from his faculty position at the American University in Beirut, Lebanon, was still the director of the survey in the 1946–47 season. Mrs. Hughes and I succumbed to the blandishments of Dr. Nelson and his designated successor, Professor Richard A. Parker, to leave the Signal Intelligence Service, where we had spent World War II, to be part of the survey staff. The survey had been entirely inoperative from the spring of 1940 to the autumn of 1946.

The late Charles F. Nims and his wife, Myrtle, also returned to the survey from his war duty in the Army Chaplain Corps at the invitation of Nelson and Parker in 1946. They had spent some time on the survey learning epigraphy in 1934 before going to the Oriental Institute Sakkarah Expedition to work on the Tomb of Mereruka. The postwar staff consisted of veterans, the Nelsons, Parkers, Nimses, Stanley Shepherd, a draftsman, and John "Tim" Healey, the engineer who had long maintained "Chicago House" (Nelson objected to that name for the home base of the survey). Only Mark Hasselriis, a draftsman, and the Hugheses were novices on the job. We thought that we could go out to Egypt for the trip, the experience, and to start up operations before assuming a teaching position in the States if we could find one.

We eventually left the survey to take up a teaching post at the Oriental Institute in Chicago in the spring of 1964, but we were replaced by John and Mary Wilson during the 1958–59 season when Carl H. Kraeling, director of the Oriental Institute, gave us a year at home. I was director of the survey from January 1, 1949 to December 31, 1963, when I turned the post over to Charles Nims. Richard Parker had been director for the 1947–48 season and half of the 1948–49 season when he left to assume his new post as Wilbour Professor of Egyptology, a newly established position at Brown University in Providence, Rhode Island.

Most of what I know about the years prior to 1946 I learned incidentally from Dr. Nelson and from W. F. Edgerton, J. A. Wilson (both of the latter were my teachers in the 1920s) and from K. Seele. They were early members of the survey in its formative years. They had collated the drawings of draftsmen like the German Bollacher and the Italian Canziani, who were early, if not the earliest, draftsmen of the survey. Edgerton had the reputation of having contributed greatly to the procedure to ensure a "definitive" copy of a relief or inscription. Seele was often said to have been the most exacting of epigraphers in his collating of drawings.

I also believe that the aforementioned staff members were among those who moved with the survey from "old" Chicago House, which was located on the west bank on the desert edge behind the Colossi of Memnon midway between Ramses II's Ramesseum and Ramses III's Medinet Habu. In 1931, the survey moved to the east side of the Nile to the present Chicago House and its luxurious quarters.

In 1946, when the Parkers, Nimses, and Hugheses journeyed from Chicago to Egypt by train and steamship, Nelson met us at Alexandria. After a night in Alexandria, while getting our luggage we entrained for Cairo where we put up at the Continental Savoy near Opera Square. That was before the center of gravity of Cairo had shifted to the present center near the Egyptian Museum and the Nile Hilton Hotel. In that immediate postwar year all transportation in Egypt was by horse-drawn carriage. The odor of the horses on the carriages lined up in front of the hotel was not appetizing as we ate our evening meals on the veranda.

When we took the night train to Luxor (that was the normal mode of travel between Cairo and Upper Egypt then), we found what the Nelsons already knew after their summer at Chicago House. When it had seemed certain that General Rommel would take Egypt as he came eastward from North Africa and the Americans would not be back, Chicago House had been looted of automobile tires, silverware, rugs, and other such usable things, but not books from the library. Nobody has ever been able to find out who was responsible, despite various rumors. Our first epigraphic work had to be done at Karnak in the Temple of Khonsu and on the Bubastite Gate, the south doorway to the open courtyard in front of the Second Pylon of the great temple. We could walk the distance to Karnak, but had no transportation to Medinet Habu, across the river.

There was, however, plenty to do at the house because there were dictionary slips to prepare and a file of the inscriptions that had been recorded before the war and a few drawings that Stan Shepherd was currently working on. Nims had photographs to take and print. The library had made no acquisitions since 1940 and, since I was the new boy on the block, I was made librarian. Catching up was not always easy, especially when we were told by dealers that the whole stock of some publications had been destroyed in the bombing of Berlin. In one case Professor Erwin Seidl sent us his own copy, because Nims and I had sent him and his family CARE parcels in the wake of World World II.

The years following 1946 saw a number of events that changed Egypt as a nation and frequently affected the survey at Luxor. They saw the driving of King Farouk into exile and the assumption of power by a junta of army officers headed first by Mohammed Naguib, who was soon ousted by Gamal Abd el-Nasser. There was the British-French-Israeli attack on Suez in 1956 and the launching of the new High Dam at Assuan. In the wake of the Suez attack, there was the "Israeli spy" scare, when we and our guests were apt to come under suspicion. For example, the brass plate on the left gate-post to the survey compound was stolen because it was in the English language. It said only "University of Chicago, The Oriental Institute, Headquarters in Egypt"; the other gate-post said the same thing, but was in Arabic. I eventually had it replaced. We also received an anonymous letter telling us to get rid of any British subjects on the staff. Our British engineer, his wife Doris, and their two small sons moved from the small house they were occupying in the garden into a suite in the "big" house as a precaution.

Egyptologically, the years following 1946 saw the replacement of French Director General of Antiquities Étienne Drioton by an Egyptian citizen, and most of the British on the staff of the Cairo Museum by Egyptian nationals as well. One of my first obligations as field director was to store the equipment of the Abydos epigraphic expedition headed by Amice Calverley. She had been given 24 hours to leave Egypt when her continuing anthropological studies in the villages of the area brought her into direct conflict with the Egyptian security police, and one morning our foreman Ibrahim came to me at breakfast to inform me that a whole boatload of her equipment had arrived without warning.

Those years also saw the establishing of the Cairo office of the American Research Center in Egypt (ARCE) under the directorship of William Stevenson Smith of the Museum of Fine Arts in Boston, who had worked before the war at Giza on the Harvard-Boston expedition under George Reisner. Smith lived at Mena House and his "office" was in his hat. Since he was in Egypt on a Fulbright Fellowship, he needed affiliation with an institution in Egypt. Since he represented an American organization, he was assigned to the Epigraphic Survey in Luxor. Before 1964 we were to see Ray Smith and John Dorman succeed Bill Smith and develop ARCE.

We of the survey were fortunate in getting an Egyptologist via Fulbright and ARCE to aid Nims and myself with epigraphy after we had been enabled by Director Kraeling to add an epigrapher to collate the drawings of the enlarged staff of draftsmen (Champion, Coleman, Greener, and Floroff). That new member was none other than Edward F. Wente, now a senior faculty member here in Chicago.

The event that drastically altered the routine of drawing and collating at Luxor was the international call via UNESCO to "save the monuments of Nubia." The survey temporarily abandoned its recording at Medinet Habu and the XVIIIth Dynasty Tomb of Kheruef to record the small Beit el-Wali temple of Ramses II in Lower Nubia. It had to be moved out of the reach of the waters of the planned High Dam at Assuan. The so-called Nubian Expedition was directed by Keith Seele, while the survey photographed and recorded the temple in the concession. Herbert Ricke of the Swiss Institute in Cairo directed excavations in the area. His wife Ursula fed and made us comfortable on our houseboat moored near the temple.

Seele and the Nubian Expedition later went further south to map and excavate in the Adindan area. But the survey had no part in the work there. In a later year Seele was in the hospital with diverticulosis and I was asked to take the Nubian Expedition to the Sudan to excavate around Serra East not far above the Sudanese-Egypt border, a site dating from Pharaonic to Coptic times. We were then joined by Ronald J. and Vivien Williams of the University of Toronto, Canada, Louis V. Žabkar of Loyola University in Chicago, and James Knudstad, who had surveyed and mapped the tomb of Kheruef in Luxor, but who had previously worked for the Oriental Institute at Nippur in Iraq. Williams and Žabkar had received their doctorates in Egyptology at the University of Chicago, so they had affinities with the Oriental Institute.

We of the survey greatly enjoyed and profited from the sojourns at Chicago House by numerous Egyptological scholars during the years 1946 to 1964. They were mainly British; only a few Americans were among them. The Germans and French seldom stayed with us. Frenchmen like Pierre Lacau, Jacques Vandier, and Jean Leclant stayed with the Henri Chevriers at Karnak, but used our library. Christiane Desroches Noblecourt and her husband André did stay with us. Bill Smith and Dows Dunham of Boston were perhaps the only American visitors, but there were eventually many non-Egyptologists who stopped over with us. One of the great characters of Egyptology was Natacha Rambova, whom we saw when her draftsman and photographer stayed with us at Chicago House while she was preparing the photographic record of the Tomb of Ramses VI in the Valley of the Kings for Alexandre Piankoff's publication of it in the Bollingen Series. To name but a few of the other Egyptologists who visited, the Britons included Sir Alan Gardiner, S. R. K. Glanville and his student H. S. Smith, Jaroslav Černý, I. E. S. Edwards, Kenneth Kitchen, and Rosalind Moss and Ethel Burney. We had provided transportation for Černý and Georges Posener to and from Deir el-Medineh to work on the ostraca for the French Institute. But our long-time neighbor and incomparable friend and collaborator in Luxor and in Nubia later was certainly Labib Habachi, who was chief inspector for Upper Egypt during my years in Egypt. Labib lived only a block from us in the Inspectorate and spent much time in the Chicago House library. His elder sister Rifka was his hostess and housekeeper. She had been looking after him since his youth. He was both a first-class scholar and a human being of rare quality.

BACKGROUND ON THE ORIENTAL INSTITUTE'S PREHISTORIC PROJECT

Robert J. and Linda S. Braidwood

Both Braidwoods performed their first field work for the Oriental Institute during the mid to late 1930s, in Syria. The Oriental Institute's Syrian excavations were in the Amouq (the Plain of Antioch, now the Turkish Hatay province). Also, for a month and a half, in 1938, we excavated on the Mediterranean coast near Tartous, Syria. In both the Amouq and at one of the coastal sites, we exposed our then earliest (ca. 5500 B.C.E.) village-farming community materials, and their implications fascinated us.

Upon returning to Chicago in late 1938, we entered graduate work at the Oriental Institute, including participation in Professor Henri Frankfort's magnificent archaeological seminar, where we both concentrated on the range of early village-farming materials. We were also involved in the processing of the early Amouq and Tartous materials for publication.

As World War II ended, Bob was involved in a new three-quarter, seminar-style course in anthropology, "Human Origins." The problem of determining the origins of a village-farming way of life increasingly interested us. Without settled, year-round communities dependent on newly domesticated plants and animals for a stable food supply, the developments of subsequent urban, literate civilization could not have followed. In retrospect, it was the Frankfort seminar, two anthropology department colleagues, Sol Tax and the late W. M. Krogman, plus warm encouragement from V. Gordon Childe (an imaginative and thoughtful British prehistorian) that most stimulated our thinking.

In the autumn of 1947, the Oriental Institute's director, Thorkild Jacobsen, provided us with encouragement and a field budget for what came to be known as the Oriental Institute's Prehistoric Project. In the spring of 1948, we made our first exposure at the site of Jarmo, in the Zagros mountains east of Kirkuk, Iraq. There were also two succeeding seasons of excavation at Jarmo (1950–51; 1954–55), and by our field colleague, Bruce Howe, at nearby still earlier sites. Now real evidence for understanding the formation of a settled, food-producing community way of life was beginning to come into our hands.

In both the second and third Jarmo seasons we were able to increase the number of our field participants dealing with the natural sciences aspects of the problem. Indeed, one of the first two field grants (and the larger of them) ever made by the National Science Foundation for archaeology was awarded to aid us in taking botanical, geological, and zoological colleagues and their assistants to the field.

We anticipated a further return to Iraq and Jarmo, but in 1958 a revolution took place, with complete loss of security in the Iraqi Zagros region. Through the interest and participation of a former Oriental Institute Iranian graduate student, Ezat Negahban, it was possible to undertake a 1959–60 field season near Kermanshah, in Iran. We made a brief exposure at a Jarmo-like early village site, Sarab, and Bruce Howe excavated in several caves and on one earlier village site, Asiab, that was in the incipient range. Again, natural scientists were with us and their results were increasingly important.

That we did not return to Iran was the result of two factors. First, there was an increasing rise of interest in the whole early village-farming community problem focus, and various younger colleagues, Canadian and Danish, as well as some Americans who were our former students, were planning Iranian excavations. Most important for us, however, was the success we had in stimulating the interest of Halet Çambel, head of the Prehistory Section of Istanbul University, in forming a "Joint Prehistoric Project of the Istanbul and Chicago Universities." We had long been fascinated by what we took to be the environmental potentials of the eastern Tauros piedmont area of Turkey—Tigris River headwater country for agricultural beginnings. We had actually sought permission to work in the region after the end of Jarmo excavations in the mid-late 1950s, but southeastern Turkey was a military zone, forbidden ground to foreigners. (Only very recently have things begun to relax somewhat.) The plan for a joint effort with Halet was, however, cleared in late 1962.

The Joint Prehistoric Project had its first field season in 1963–64, beginning with a broad-ranging surface survey, in order to locate a site of the time range of our interest. The surface yield of a site called Çayönü Tepesi, in the Ergani plain, northwest of the city of Diyarbakir, was our choice for excavation, which we began in the succeeding spring, 1964. There have been 12 more field seasons at Çayönü since that first one. Çayönü was, indeed, a very impressive early village-farming community site, with a cluster of radiocarbon age determinations that (recalibrated) span the time range of ca. 10,400 to 9,800 years ago. Çayönü was, however, already well up on the threshold of a settled food-producing way of life. A greater question still remains: what exactly went on during a preceding range of incipience when the first steps toward the domestication of plants and animals were taking place?

Although an excellent younger Turkish colleague, Mehmet Özdogan, is now continuing at Çayönü, Halet and we, and our German architectural colleague, Wulf Schirmer (head of the Institut für Baugeschichte at Karlsruhe University), agreed that the 1988 season must be our last **as excavators** (actual earth-movers) at Çayönü. There remains a very **heavy** load of report writing, for which we share moral responsibility. There is also an added complication: since antiquities may not be exported from Turkey, the processing for final reports must all be done in Istanbul.

In retrospect, concerning the Oriental Institute's Prehistoric Project's activities, we do feel greatly gratified over the amount of raw evidence we have been able to acquire. It concerns a moment of very great change in the human career. And we also feel very pleased that so many younger archaeological colleagues both here and abroad (many of them students from Chicago or Istanbul) have been drawn into the problem focus. The increasingly standard addition of natural scientists to such field programs is also a firm step forward. We feel most fortunate to have had a part in stimulating attention toward this very important part of the human past.

REFERENCES

Braidwood, R. J.
1986 The Origin and Growth of a Research Focus—Agricultural Beginnings. *Expedition* 28 (no. 2): 2–6.

Braidwood, L. S. and R. J. Braidwood
1986 Prelude to the Appearance of Village-Farming Communities in Southwestern Asia. In J. Vorys Canby et al., *Ancient Anatolia: Aspects of Change and Cultural Development.* Madison, Wisconsin.

Braidwood, L. S.
1983 *Prehistoric Archaeology Along the Zagros Flanks.* Oriental Institute Publication 105. Chicago.

ORIENTAL INSTITUTE EXCAVATIONS AT KHORSABAD, IRAQ (1929–1935)

Karen L. Wilson

IN the early spring of 1920, James Henry Breasted, the founder and first director of the Oriental Institute, visited the site of Khorsabad (Figs. 1 and 2) for the first time. There he confirmed the impression that he had already gained from reading French archaeologists' publications of their mid-19th century excavations at Dur Sharrukin: there was still a great deal of archaeological work to be done in the capital city of King Sargon II (ca. 721–705 B.C.E.). Breasted wrote:

> the entire site, including the mounds, was under cultivation by the natives, who had been raising grain on the ruins of Sargon's capital for many, many centuries. ... The palace has entirely disappeared since the French excavations, but in following the line of the extensive walls we found that the gates, of which there were several on each side, had been structures of monumental architecture. Though now grass-grown hills, each of the gates could be excavated with great profit, for the natives uncovered in our presence a large alabaster threshold in one of the gates, bearing impressive cuneiform records of the campaigns of Sargon, the conqueror of Samaria, and the Assyrian king who carried away the captives of the Ten Tribes of Israel and exiled them. ... There were many rumors of sculptures lying just below the surface among the palace mounds, but the brevity of our visit made it impossible to verify these reports.

Nevertheless, Breasted came away determined to excavate the city.

Some years later, Professor Edward Chiera, newly appointed to the University of Chicago, also visited Khorsabad. On his arrival, the villagers uncovered for him a fragment of relief showing two magnificent horses' heads, thus confirming the presence of treasures lying just beneath the cultivation. After obtaining a concession for the site, the Oriental Institute's newly constituted Assyrian Expedition began work early in 1929, with Chiera as field director. They quickly discovered that the sculptures that Paul Émile Botta and Victor Place had seen and recorded in the mid-19th century had suffered frightful destruction during the intervening decades. This was because for the first time in over 1,000 years the stones had been exposed—to both the natural elements and the quarrying activities of local villagers, who burned the sculptures for lime and cut them into pieces to use as building blocks and milling stones.

The site of Khorsabad takes its name from a village that stands on the ruins of an ancient city called Dur Sharrukin ("Fort Sargon"). That city was constructed, on what appears to have been land not previously occupied, as a new capital by King Sargon shortly after he came to the throne of Assyria in 721 B.C.E. Although the city was formally dedicated in 706 B.C.E., it had not been completed when Sargon died the following year. His son and successor, Sennacherib, moved the Assyrian capital to the old established city of Nineveh, about 15 miles to the south, and Dur Sharrukin appears to have been almost completely abandoned.

During his initial season, Chiera uncovered what may have been the best preserved of the reliefs that were still standing in Sargon's palace—in Corridor 10 and Court VIII (Fig. 3). In fact, Chiera's letters to Breasted reveal an expedition beset by an enviable problem—they were finding too much. For example, on 29 March 1929, Chiera wrote: "We could of course go on excavating for another month, but then we would have much more in our hands than we could ship." And his problems had only just begun. Early in April, workmen in Court VIII uncovered fragments of a human-headed winged bull, which had fallen face downward onto the pavement, had then been covered with the debris of the falling building, and was thus perfectly preserved, albeit broken into a considerable number of pieces. Chiera was uncertain what to do with this new discovery and immediately cabled Breasted: "FOUND WINGED BULL FIVE METERS BY FIVE FACE TURNING SIDE WAYS GOOD CONDITION STOP SHIPPING POSSIBLE MONTH MAY ONLY STOP COST TRANSPORTATION ABOUT TEN THOUSAND DOLLARS STOP DIVISION APRIL TWENTY SIXTH STOP SHALL WE ASK FOR BULL." In a letter written the same day, he explained that although the bull was broken into pieces, even these fragments were too large to be shipped by truck and would have to be floated down the Tigris, which would be at high level only during May. Breasted promptly cabled Chiera to ask for the piece during the division and to make all necessary arrangements to transport the bull to Chicago, even though he had no money in his budget with which to foot the bill.

Finances, however, proved to be a minor problem in the saga of the shipping of the bull, which began as a close-in race against time and the falling waters of the Tigris and was a constant struggle, all the way from Khorsabad to Hyde Park, against the sheer mass of the pieces. Each of the large fragments into which the bull had broken had to be lifted from its resting place by locally made hoists and then required a wooden case, reinforced with iron beams, built around it. Once the pieces had been crated, it took 15 days to travel the 12 miles to the river, for the only vehicle available to carry the largest fragment was woefully inadequate for the task and broke down repeatedly. In the end, the truck collapsed about 300 meters from the river, which was falling at such a rapid rate that no time could be spent on repairs. The disabled vehicle thus had to be dragged by steel cables the remaining distance to the waiting boat. Three days were spent maneuvering the crate onto the deck (Fig. 4), another in pulling the boat (which was now partially aground due to the added weight and the rapidly falling water level) back into the river, and the bull was at last on its way. Three years after its discovery, when the bull had been reconstructed and safely installed in the brand-new Oriental Institute building (Fig. 5), a local newspaper columnist wrote: "The forty-ton bull of King Sargon II, after three years of travel, finally has been tethered permanently. 'And thank goodness for that,' sighed Dr. Edward Chiera today."

So great was the embarrassment of all these riches, that after the end of the first season Chiera suggested that the Oriental Institute take up work at another site. "An excavation in Khorsabad only would not be good for the prestige of the Institute," he wrote to Breasted from the field. "While all institutions take their chances on new sites, we do not want to show that we invest our funds mainly to get things, and to get them where we are certain to find them." Consequently, the Assyrian Expedition was subsumed into the larger Iraq Expedition, which began excavations in the Diyala Region the same year. However, future seasons at Khorsabad proved beyond a doubt the scientific value of continued work at the site.

On 26 January 1930, the Iraq Expedition resumed investigations in the city of Sargon under the direction of Henri Frankfort. One of their architects, Gordon Loud, was placed in charge of the Khorsabad excavations later that year and was to lead five more seasons before the Oriental Institute Khorsabad Expedition came to a close in 1935. The tenor of these seasons was very different from the initial one. The expedition never encountered the wealth of large stone sculptures that Chiera had stumbled upon, but continued to unearth significant fresh information on the site.

Because much of Sargon's new capital city had never been finished, let alone inhabited, and because it was abandoned in a leisurely manner, there were few small finds during any season. Most of the new information gained concerned the architecture: the plans, methods of construction and decoration, and the functions of those public buildings that had been the first to be built at the site (the city walls, palace, official residences, and temples).

Frankfort began work at the city gate that had been numbered 7 by Place (Fig. 2)—the only town gate that had not been excavated at least partly by him. Work revealed that this entrance into the city had apparently never been used, but had been walled up soon after its construction. Many details were observed here that had not been recorded before at Dur Sharrukin. The interior of the gate had been whitewashed, as had all of the interior and exterior brickwork, and the gate had been roofed with beams covered with mats and mud, all of which had been painted red.

During this second season the excavators also turned their attention to the palace and an area within it that Place had called Court VII (Fig. 3). They believed that this room, which was entered from Court VIII through three imposing gates elaborately decorated with winged human-headed bulls (including the one now in the Oriental Institute Museum), would prove to be more important than a second courtyard. This was, indeed, the case: they had discovered nothing less than the throne room of King Sargon. Sufficient evidence of decayed beams survived to prove that the room had been covered over and was not a court, as Place had reported. The patterns decorating the plaster laid over the beams and patterns in colored plaster that had apparently covered the upper parts of the walls, above the row of relief slabs, were studied, copied, and restored in color renderings, making an entirely new contribution to contemporary knowledge of Assyrian architectural decoration: a painted procession of life-sized figures had adorned the walls **above** the reliefs.

While these excavations were going on, Pinhas Delougaz, who had so masterfully supervised the transportation of the bull, was assigned the job of removing and packing the carved slabs that Chiera had found in Room 7 of the palace. While engaged in this task, he discovered a surprising method of construction in this relatively small room: the relief slabs had been erected before the mudbrick walls themselves were constructed and had been carved in place.

During the third season (1931–32), the expedition returned to the palace to investigate a large quarter in its southern corner, which Place had called the "harem" but which a German archaeologist, Walter Andrae, had recognized from the plans to be a group of temples. The discovery of inscribed stone doorsills bearing the names of the deities Sin, Shamash, Ningal, Adad, Ninurta, and Ea confirmed Andrae's theory. Everywhere the excavators found evidence of work halted on buildings upon the death of Sargon: thresholds of doorways that had never been put into place and pivot-stones not yet covered by the large paving slabs with cut-outs that sat unbroken on the surrounding pavements ready to be lowered into position. They also discovered evidence of work unsupervised or poorly supervised: many of the foundation deposit boxes had been sealed and buried devoid of the contents that would have made them efficacious.

While work proceeded on the temples, two separate areas within the town were excavated in the hope of obtaining some information about Assyrian private houses. The excavators knew from their work near Gate 7 that large areas within the town had never been inhabited, but conjectured that there were two parts of the city that would have been settled first: the southeastern quarter of the town, which was situated immediately behind the gate through which those coming from the bustling city of Nineveh would pass; and the area near the palace and temples. Walks through the plowed fields that covered the city showed potsherds intermingled with soil in both these areas, and trenches were opened where the sherds were most thickly strewn. The southern trial trench revealed the existence of walls founded on layers of stones and large pebbles, but the floor of the building seemed to be almost level with the surface. It also seemed fairly certain that this had been a public building, rather than a private house, as its construction included stone doorsills and bricks stamped with the name of Sargon.

In the second area, between Gate 1 and the palace, three trenches reached virgin soil without revealing any traces of architecture, although the ground contained habitation debris throughout its depth of about two meters. It appeared to Frankfort that whatever private houses had existed at the site may have been so insubstantial as to leave no trace after being subjected to centuries of annual plowing. Therefore, the search for domestic structures was abandoned and the work of future seasons concentrated upon the area of the palace and temples.

By the end of the fourth season at Khorsabad, it had become obvious to the members of the Iraq Expedition that the short seasons they had been spending at the site—tacked onto the ends of full seasons at Eshnunna, when the sand storms and heat drove them from the Diyala Region—were not sufficient for the excavation of a city built on such a massive scale. Therefore, in 1932, Gordon Loud was appointed field director of the Khorsabad Expedition by Dr. Frankfort and worked at the site for three 4–6-month seasons in 1932–33, 1933–34, and 1934–35.

Working through the winters at Khorsabad was unexpectedly difficult due to persistent driving rains, but the expedition staff appears to have consisted of true pioneers. On 7 February 1933, Loud wrote in the field diary, "We have no firewood at present except what we cut from the roofbeams of the old living room—those which were too worm-eaten and cracked to be re-used—for in this weather no donkeys bring their wood down our way." And, on the following day he wrote, "What an event: a full day's work on the dig. True, it wasn't without a few drops of rain, but what an improvement just the same. I look forward to the novelty of walking upon dry ground—such hasn't happened for nearly a month now." And sometimes rain was not the worst of their difficulties as attested to by this entry on 17 January 1934: "A week of almost continual interruptions. Rain began while we were in Mosul last Thursday evening and continued in its usual intermittent fashion until a fall of snow Sunday morning put an end to it."

Despite the elements, however, the three seasons were tremendously productive because of the careful excavation of the area immediately south of Sargon's palace, most of which had never before been investigated. During a previous season, while working around Gate 1, Loud had written: "I should like a wall extending around the palace mound within the town. Such an idea comes to me from the topography of the surface as it is today. I should like a wall extending around this part of the palace with a gate directly opposite the main palace entrance at a spot where a considerable mound now exists." Two years later, he got what he had wished for, and his hunch was confirmed that the entire area south of the palace had been enclosed by its own wall, so that it formed a kind of citadel with the palace itself. Within this wall, standing on its own platform, was the Nabu Temple, which was surrounded in turn by what must have been the residences of Sargon's highest officials, labeled simply by the excavators, "Residences K, L, J, and M." Only the owner of Residence L could be identified: Sinahusur, Sargon's brother and grand vizier.

One of the citadel gates, its walls faced with magnificently preserved limestone reliefs of winged genii, standing behind the customary guardian human-headed winged bulls, was exposed in February of 1934. This time a division of the sculptures was denied. They were transported to Baghdad by the director general of antiquities in 1938–39 and now stand proudly in the Assyrian Halls of the Iraq Museum.

Work at the site was brought to a close in April of 1935. On 25 February 1935, Loud had written to Breasted, "I now feel convinced that we can abandon the site with a clear conscience at the end of the season, providing we complete the plan of the citadel. The city can be dug completely at enormous expense and, I believe, without results to warrant it. We must therefore stop somewhere. ..."

Loud left Khorsabad for the last time on 10 May 1935, to become field director of the institute's excavations at Megiddo. The significance of the results of his last three seasons, in terms of their contribution to our knowledge and understanding of Neo-Assyrian architecture, cannot be too heavily stressed, and the publication he produced less than three years later sets them forth in enviable detail.

REFERENCES

Botta, P. E. and E. Flandin
1849–50 *Monument de Ninive.* Five vols. Paris.

Breasted, J. H.
1933 *The Oriental Institute.* The University of Chicago Survey Volume XII. Chicago.

Loud, G.
1936 *Khorsabad Part I. Excavations in the Palace and at a City Gate.* Oriental Institute Publications Volume 38. Chicago.

Loud, G. and C. B. Altman
1938 *Khorsabad Part II. The Citadel and the Town.* Oriental Institute Publications Volume 40. Chicago.

Oriental Institute Archives
1929–35 Unpublished sources in the Director's Office Correspondence Files; Khorsabad field diaries.

Place, V.
1867–70 *Ninive et l'Assyrie.* Paris.

GEORGE ERNEST WRIGHT AND THE SHECHEM EXPEDITION

Edward F. Campbell

ONE of Chicago's many bases for archaeological research is McCormick Theological Seminary. The tradition began with George L. Robinson, who explored Petra in 1900 and discovered the "High Place" there, then chronicled Petra in his 1930 book, *The Sarcophagus of an Ancient Civilization.* It continued in the 1920s and 1930s with Ovid R. Sellers, excavator of Beth-zur and Silet edh-Dhahr; and from 1938 to 1958 with G. Ernest Wright. It currently continues on through Robert G. Boling and Edward F. Campbell. All were/are members of the Chicago Society of the Archaeological Institute of America. Sellers was its secretary for many years. Wright also had the honor to serve as president of the American Schools for Oriental Research.

The focus of McCormick's archaeological program lies with the work at Tell Balatah, the site of ancient Shechem, located on the eastern edge of Nablus in the modern West Bank Territory, deep in the valley between Mt. Ebal and Mt. Gerizim. The genius of the McCormick roster was G. Ernest Wright, who fielded the Shechem dig in conjunction with Dean Bernhard W. Anderson of Drew University in Madison, New Jersey. The Drew-McCormick association added eleven other schools to form a consortium that was in the field 1956 to 1969, with minor salvage operations in 1972–73. Wright towered over the project, but he meanwhile launched expeditions under leaders he trained at Shechem, notably at Taanach, Gezer, Idalion (Cyprus), and Hesi. Furthermore, he had assumed the presidency of the American Schools of Oriental Research in 1965, a position that he held, now from his base at Harvard University, until his death in 1974.

What Wright wanted to do at Shechem was to train a new generation of archaeological researchers in the post-Second World War era. His approach was to meticulously separate soil layers controlled by standing balks at the edges of digging plots, the method developed by Dame Kathleen Kenyon, and combine it with W. F. Albright's keen attention to ceramic typology. Wright had already contributed to ceramic typology by means of his own studies in Early Bronze Age pottery for his doctoral dissertation at Johns Hopkins. Archaeological interpretation thus became a conversation between stratigraphy and typology. Two other commitments played crucial parts in the research plan for Shechem. One was Wright's work in biblical theology, which had led him to wrestle with early traditions in the Bible about important events taking place at Shechem, notably, Abraham's association with it (Genesis 12:6–7), the covenant renewal ceremony presented in Joshua 24 and the conflicts over kingship reflected in Judges 9 and I Kings 12—not to mention the question of the part Shechem and its region played in the life of the Samaritans. The other was Wright's growing sensitivity to the role the physical and social sciences would come to play in archaeological research. Here his resource was the Henri Frankfort Prehistoric Seminar at the Oriental Institute and his association with the vision of Robert and Linda Braidwood. It was Wright's intent to take a geologist with him to the early Shechem campaigns—a plan repeatedly frustrated until 1968. He often spoke of "deficient curiosity on the part of excavators," and sought to overcome that deficiency by associating with digs as many broad-visioned researchers in the sciences as was feasible.

What did Wright and his colleagues find at Shechem? First of all, a previously dug site. An Austro-German expedition had worked there beginning in 1913–14, continuing in the twenties and winding up in 1934. The work had not been well supervised, and, far more devastating, virtually all the records and many key artifacts had been destroyed in the Allied bombing of Berlin in 1943. Only preliminary reports had been published, and some of these were so skimpy as to be useless. But a lot of dirt had been moved. As a result, it was possible to spend half of the Americans' effort clarifying already-visible fortifications surrounding the approximately 16-acre site, as well as the public buildings in the city's acropolis. Fortifications defining Shechem as a major Middle Bronze Age Canaanite city-state were first erected around 1750 B.C.E. and successively renewed, reconceived, and strengthened until the whole city was demolished around 1540 B.C.E., assumedly in connection with the expulsion of the Hyksos by the incoming Eighteenth Egyptian Dynasty. Two rather well-preserved city gate structures, go with substantial portions of the preserved walls to make the site an outdoor museum to this day. Subsequent fortifications simply reconstructed these MB II antecedents.

Even more striking is the massive temple structure belonging to MB IIC (1650–1540) on the acropolis along the western perimeter of the town. It is 26.30 × 21.20 meters in size with foundation walls 5.10 meters thick. On top of it were the scant remains of a Late Bronze Age structure, oriented slightly off the axis of the earlier building, which seems to be a broad-roomed temple dating across the period

1450 to 1100. Both the MB IIC and the LB structures had altars and standing stones in the courtyard in front of them—the sort of furnishings that led Wright to reaffirm what his German predecessor Sellin had posited: that the pictures in Joshua 24:25–27 and Judges 9 had their roots in phenomena at Shechem of just this sort.

Beneath this massive "fortress temple" or *migdal* lay a complex of public buildings, which for a time was thought to represent in its totality another temple system. Wright published this as a succession of MB IIB "courtyard temples." More recently, both the excavation team and other archaeological interpreters have analyzed the complex instead as a multi-use set of public buildings, probably including a palace and a sanctuary, the sort of combination that would characterize an acropolis. Regrettably, it would require the demolition of the preserved migdal to bring greater clarity into this picture. There is no doubt, however, that this whole part of town was separated off from "downtown" Shechem by a precinct wall. Deep below the acropolis, evidence of settlement belonging to Chalcolithic times lies on bedrock; the only indication of Early Bronze Age settlement is a rather large representation of EB pottery in fills throughout the site.

The other half of the American effort involved tracing the site's stratigraphy from the surface down, conducting a thorough regional survey of the Shechem plain, and exploring remarkable structures on Tell er-Ras, the prominent spur of Mt. Gerizim which rises just to the south of the city. All in all, the city itself had 24 strata, from its beginnings in Chalcolithic until late in the second century B.C.E.—ending with the destruction wrought by John Hyrcanus. Domestic housing of the Late Bronze and Iron ages provides important evidence for reconstructing the social history of a Canaanite and Israelite town, including a very well-preserved Israelite "four-room" house of the eighth century torched by the invading Assyrian army around 724 B.C.E. Four strata of Hellenistic occupation probably represent the development here, at the foot of the Samaritans' sacred mountain, Gerizim, of a city to replace Samaria in the wake of Alexander the Great's activities there. During this time, it appears that a massive foundation for a Samaritan tabernacle-style sanctuary was erected on Tell er-Ras, later to be consolidated into the podium for a Greek-style temple by Hadrian's engineers and architects in the second century C.E.

Excavation at Shechem ceased with the Hague Convention agreements on archaeological work in occupied territories implemented in 1968–69. The expedition now toils at its publication responsibilities.

REFERENCES

Bull, R. J. and E. F. Campbell, Jr.
1968 The Sixth Campaign at Balâtah. *BASOR* 190: 2–41.

Wright, E. G.
1936 Chronology of Palestine in the Early Bronze Age. *BASOR* 63: 12–21.
1938 Chronology of Palestine in the Middle Bronze Age. *BASOR* 71: 27–35.
1956 The First Campaign at Tell Balâtah (Schechem). *BASOR* 144: 9–20.
1957 The Second Campaign at Tell Balâtah (Schechem). *BASOR* 148: 11–28.
1958 Comment on Yadin's Dating of the Schechem Temple. *BASOR* 150: 34–36.
1959 Israelite Samaria and Iron Age Chronology. *BASOR* 155: 13–20.
1961 The Third Campaign at Tell Balâtah. *BASOR* 161: 11–55.
1962 Selected Seals from the Excavations at Balâtah (Schechem). *BASOR* 167: 5–14.
1963 The Fourth Campaign at Balâtah. *BASOR* 169:1–61.
1965 The Fifth Campaign at Balâtah. *BASOR* 180: 7–41.

RECENT INDICATIONS OF HELLENIZATION AT ANCIENT SEPPHORIS (LOWER GALILEE), ISRAEL

Dennis E. Groh

THE long history of the Chicago Society's involvement in Palestinian archaeology continues with the present excavation work in Galilee. Earlier generations of scholars had regarded Jewish assimilation to Greco-Roman language, artistic conventions, and values to be based on a broad geographical distinction: Jews who lived within the Holy Land were less Hellenized than Jcws who lived in Diaspora among the Gentile regions of the Empire. While preserving some clear distinction between Diaspora and Holy Land Jews, the last generation of scholars had begun a radical reappraisal of the older picture and had begun to indicate the incorporation of a great number of Gentile religious motifs and practices into the synagogue life of late antique Palestine. Thus, scholars of the present generation, in both text studies and archaeology, tend to discuss Palestinian Judaism in terms of **degrees** of Hellenization or assimilation.

In this regard, recent research has detailed two differing kinds of Judaism in late antiquity. The period of the 3rd and 4th centuries (ca. 250–361 C.E.) has emerged as one of the densely settled and prosperous periods in Galilean history, and it is precisely in this time period that we are able to trace the outline of two differing regional kinds of Judaism.

Eric Meyers, based on Josephus' distinction, has given us a picture of an Upper Galilean and a Lower Galilean Judaism. It is Lower Galilee with which we are concerned in this presentation, for Sepphoris is one of the region's two great cities.

Lower Galilee's northern extent is constituted by the plain of Galilee and the area of the sea as far north as a line running from Chorazin west through Beer-Sheva to the north. Jewish synagogue remains in the region show a high degree of familiarity with Greco-Roman artistic conventions. The synagogue excavated at Hammath Tiberias is a good example of Lower Galilean Judaism in late antiquity: a representational zodiac adorns the central nave of the synagogue; entryway and aisles contain a predominance of Greek inscriptions; Hebrew, where it appears, is slight and miswritten; one Aramaic inscription decorates an aisle. This building of a predominately Greek-speaking Jewish congregation of the early 4th century C.E. shows us both how securely Jewish and how deeply Hellenized Jews of Lower Galilee could be.

Yet no one expected the excavations at ancient Sepphoris, 18 kilometers away, to turn up such an amazing presence of pagan motifs and objects. Both the joint Duke University and Hebrew University excavations, directed by Eric M. Meyers and Ehud Netzer, and the University of South Florida excavations, directed by James F. Strange, have uncovered both small objects and large mosaics with decidedly pagan themes. Sepphoris' history as the center of rabbinic Judaism in the late 2nd–early 3rd centuries, when the oral tradition of Judaism (the Mishna) was codified, and its place as the most frequently mentioned city after Jerusalem in ancient Jewish literary sources led me and others to suppose that the city would have a less obvious Hellenistic and pagan presence. Once again, the new discoveries show us how closely even pious Jews in Lower Galilee lived with the crosscurrents of Greco-Roman Hellenism.

Small bronze figurines of pagan cultic significance have been found in cisterns by both excavations. Meyers, Meyers, and Netzer found both a Pan and a Prometheus figurine and Strange's team discovered a small bronze head of a bull that probably has Serapis associations.

However, it is in the polychrome mosaics that are coming to light that one best sees the late classical tradition and its motifs emerging at Sepphoris. In 1987, Meyers, Meyers, and Netzer discovered a large polychrome Dionysiac mosaic with panels depicting banqueting and processional scenes within a public building built in the 3rd century. The execution, especially of one portrait of a woman, renders it among the finest of mosaics ever found in the land of Israel. Greek words meaning "drunkenness" and "procession" appear in the mosaic. Located on a central spot of the acropolis of the city, the mosaic shows us a more highly profiled pagan presence than we expected, as well as a taste for finely executed Greco-Roman mosaics.

That such a find was not to be regarded as confined to a single dwelling of the city was demonstrated when a sister mosaic, though without human representational panels, was discovered this past summer by Strange, Longstaff, and Groh in field V of the Sepphoris Excavations of the University of South Florida.

The newly discovered mosaic is only partially excavated from a late Roman peristyle house. Coins found in the floor of the mosaic indicate an early 4th century (Constantinian) usage. According to our mosaic specialist, Dr. Lucille Roussin of Sarah Lawrence College, stylistically the mosaic belongs to a workshop of the city of Antioch after ca. 250 C.E. The mosaic portrays two small birds in panels and characteristic Antiochene late floral decoration. Neither the entire plan of the mosaic nor the chronological extent of its usage in antiquity is yet completely understood. The peristyle house seems to have continued in use into the Arab period, but the late plan and occupations have been disturbed by modern surface intrusions.

The excavations of ancient Sepphoris are only at the halfway point in terms of the Sepphoris Excavations' plans. But at this point Sepphoris seems to further illustrate how very comfortable with late Greco-Roman traditions and artistic conventions the Jews of Lower Galilee were, even in one of the most famous of the rabbinic and Talmudic city-sites.

REFERENCES

Dothan, M.
1983 *Hammath Tiberias*. Jerusalem.

Groh, D. E.
1988 Jews and Christians in Late Roman Palestine. Towards a New Chronology. *Biblical Archaeologist* 51(2): 80–96.

Meyers, E. M. and J.F. Strange
1981 *Archaeology, the Rabbis, and Early Christianity*. Nashville.

Meyers, E. M. et al.
1986 Sepphoris, Ornament of All Galilee. *Biblical Archaeologist* 49(1): 4–18.

Meyers, E. M. et al.
1987 Artistry in Stone. The Mosaics of Ancient Sepphoris. *Biblical Archaeologist* 50(1): 223–31.

EXCAVATIONS AT ISTHMIA AND THE WORK OF OSCAR BRONEER

Elizabeth R. Gebhard

INSPIRED by the chance appearance of a gold earring and led on by his own practical instincts, Oscar Broneer discovered the Temple of Poseidon on the Isthmus of Corinth in the spring of 1952. So began the work that was to occupy the next 25 years of a long and active life devoted to Greek archaeology. Through excavation, numerous reports and articles and, finally, the first three volumes of the final publications in the *Isthmia* series, Oscar Broneer slowly and painstakingly unraveled the long and complex history of Poseidon's famous sanctuary. Until then the site had eluded detection. It was the last of the four great Panhellenic shrines to remain lost to the modern world, since the holy places of Olympia, Delphi, and Nemea had long been recognized and placed under excavation.

The archaeological career of Oscar Broneer never followed an orthodox path. Born in a Swedish village on 28 December 1894, he worked as a lumberjack in the nearly forests before coming to America and to Chicago at the age of 17. Speaking no English, he went to work in a piano factory while attending night school to obtain a high school diploma. His natural talent for learning, and especially for languages, encouraged him to pursue a B.A. at Augustana College. The next step was a scholarship to the University of California at Berkeley. Finally, in 1924, the die was cast for his future when he won a traveling fellowship to the American School of Classical Studies in Athens. There he remained for many years as student, research archaeologist, and professor of archaeology.

Broneer's interest in the Sanctuary of Poseidon was first aroused by an inscription he found while directing excavations in Corinth. The stone commemorated the benefactions of one Lucius Priscus Iuventianus, a wealthy Corinthian of the 2nd century C.E.; it also mentioned Iuventianus' works at the Isthmian shrine. Later, during the Second World War, when many American archaeologists gathered in Princeton to continue their studies since they were not able to work in Greece, Broneer and his friends agreed that the most important Greek site still to be located was the Sanctuary of Poseidon at Isthmia.

A few years later when, as a professor at the University of Chicago, he was charged to find a suitable Greek site for a Chicago excavation, Broneer thought of the lost Sanctuary of Isthmian Poseidon. With the help of Krysoula Kardara, then a doctoral student, he examined the remains of a late antique fortification built from blocks that had assuredly belonged to a large Greek temple. Earlier travelers and archaeologists had placed the Sanctuary of Poseidon within the fortress, imagining that its walls replaced an earlier tememos boundary around the temple. A modern church to St. John the Forerunner supported their thinking, since it is well known that Christian shrines often replaced their pagan predecessors.

Broneer, on the other hand, had a different idea. He believed that the topography of the place, the lay of the land, was a better guide to the location of ancient remains. As he used to say, "The Greeks weren't silly. If we are to understand where they placed their walls and temples, we must look at the best site for such a construction." This was the reasoning that had led him earlier to find the west wall of the fortifications around the city of Corinth in the face of opposition from older and presumably wiser heads of the archaeological establishment. Now he set out to see where near the Isthmus the Corinthians most likely would have placed their great temple. It was while walking carefully over every inch of ground in the area that he climbed a low ridge, known locally as the Rachi. From there he surveyed the broken terrain below, and while doing so he realized that the only level plateau of rock suitable for the site of a major temple lay below the ridge where he was standing.

At the same time that Broneer was carefully reasoning out the topographical problems, the goddess of chance also took part in his explorations. As he looked about the bare rock that formed the top of the Rachi, he spied a gold earring, lost by some Hellenistic lady in the 3rd century B.C.E. There was no logical connection between a chance, surface find such as this and the lost Temple of Poseidon, but Broneer took it as a sign, an omen of good fortune to come.

His hopes were not in vain. Shortly afterward he laid out his first, long trench across the plateau that he had seen from the Rachi and immediately discovered the lost Temple of Poseidon. The goddess, however, never sends unmixed blessings to the race of men, and Broneer at once understood why others had looked for Poseidon's shrine for so long without success. From what had been a splendid Doric temple of the 5th century B.C.E. only the bare foundation trenches remained. Almost every wall block and column had been cut up and carried off to build the late Roman fortifications.

A lesser man then might have decided that only a limited exploration of the site was worthwhile because he was unlikely to find the artistic treasures that once had enriched the sanctuary. At that time the need for excavations to uncover many beautiful things still haunted directors, who usually depended solely on private donors or museums for support. The advent of the National Endowment for the Humanities has done much to alleviate that situation, although research grants for excavations carried out on foreign soil are still given only as matching funds for private donations. Broneer did not have much financial support, but he did have a very good understanding of the historical significance of his discoveries at the Isthmia. His passion in expounding the remains inspired many to contribute to his field work and then to give funds for a museum at the site. With the collaboration of Robert Scranton, his successor at the University of Chicago and the director of excavations at the nearby Corinthian harbor of Kenchreai, Broneer raised about $100,000 for the museum, which was then given to the Greek government. I became director of the University of Chicago Excavations at Isthmia in 1976, and my first task was that of arranging the displays and storerooms so that the museum could open to the public in 1978.

During the years 1952–67 Broneer directed six full campaigns at Isthmia and several shorter ones that uncovered the center portion of the sanctuary, the theater, two stadia, and a Hellenistic community on the Rachi, where he had originally found the prophetic earring. The Classical Temple of Poseidon, preceded by an earlier one on the same site, dominated the shrine. Around it the Romans built a series of stoas and a sanctuary to the boy-hero Melikertes-Palaimon, who shared Poseidon's holy place as patron of the Panhellenic Isthmian Games. An early stadium was built in the 6th century B.C.E. for the contests, and when the crowds who flocked to the games had increased to the point where they could no longer be accommodated in the old place, a second stadium was built in a valley nearby. Broneer restored the unique starting gates for the early racetrack and entertained many visitors with a demonstration of how runners left the post. The festival to Poseidon, held biennially in the spring, was not dedicated solely to athletic events, but it also included contests for poets and singers. For these events a theater was laid out in the 5th century, not far from the temple. I supervised excavations there and published the results in a volume on the Isthmian theater. To the west lay a gymnasium complex, including a swimming pool, buried under a bath of Roman date. An unusual pair of caves with dining couches, one near the temple and the other above the theater, accommodated special visitors during the festival. The chambers may have belonged to the cult of Demeter or to that of Dionysos, both of which are known to have been associated with Poseidon. A full kitchen, with its complement of pots and pans, made it possible for Broneer to recreate the scene of feasting that would have taken place during the festival.

Oscar Broneer lives today in Ancient Corinth and this past December he celebrated his 95th birthday. His health is good and except for the loss of his eyesight he continues much as ever, interested in the world around him, Greek politics and, of course, the latest news from the ongoing work in the Isthmian sanctuary.

A long season of excavations took place this past year under my direction and under the auspices of the University of Chicago and the American School of Classical Studies at Athens. They were supported by a grant from the National Endowment for the Humanities that matched contributions from private donors. Much new information toward reconstructing the history of the sanctuary was revealed by the exploration of the stratigraphy and monuments surrounding and including the Temple of Poseidon. We found remains that helped explain the formation of the cult place about 1100 B.C.E. and its development in succeeding centuries. Through the well-documented account of the layers of earth surrounding its central area and a detailed record of the artifacts deposited in those layers, we will be able to provide a much fuller account of the sanctuary's history. When the samples of ash, bone, carbonized plant remains, and pollen are analyzed, they will also give us information about the environment. On the Rachi, in the small community discovered by Broneer, further excavation provided evidence for the architecture of individual workshop complexes and the organization of the entire area. The pottery recovered from both the sanctuary and Rachi settlement is important for the general chronology of the Corinthia, from the Ice Age through the Roman period. Questions concerning stratigraphy and ceramics analysis, then, formed the goals of the excavations of 1989. Because they were successful, we look forward to many seasons of study based on the rich material from Poseidon's famous shrine. We feel this is the most fitting tribute to Oscar Broneer's illustrious career in classical archaeology and his pioneering work at the Isthmian Sanctuary.

REFERENCES

Broneer, O.

1953 Isthmia Excavations, 1952. *Hesperia* 22: 182–209.

1955 Excavations at Isthmia, 1954. *Hesperia* 24: 110–141.

1956 North Slope Crater: New Fragments. *Hesperia* 25: 345–50.

1958 Excavations at Isthmia, the Third Campaign. *Hesperia* 27: 1–38.

1959 Excavations at Isthmia, the Fourth Campaign. *Hesperia* 28: 298–343.

1962 Excavations at Isthmia, 1959–1960. *Hesperia*, 31: 1, 1–26.

1971 *The Temple of Poseidon, Isthmia*, I. Princeton.

1973 *Topography and Architecture, Isthmia*, II. Princeton.

Gebhard, E. R.

1973 *The Theatre at Isthmia*. Chicago.

Gregory, T.

1990 *The Hexamilion and Fortress, Isthmia*, V. (Forthcoming). Princeton.

Rostoker, W. and E. Gebhard

1983 The Sanctuary of Poseidon at Isthmia: Techniques of Metal Manufacture. *Hesperia* 49: 347–63.

Sturgeon, M.

1987 *Isthmia*, IV. *The Sculpture*. Princeton.

KENCHREAI, EASTERN PORT OF CORINTH

Hector Williams

Kenchreai, eastern port of the ancient Greek metropolis of Corinth, lies in the lee of a headland at the end of the Saronic Gulf, a little over an hour and a half drive from modern Athens. From 1963 to 1968, excavations carried out under the general direction of Professor Robert L. Scranton of the University of Chicago and under the auspices of the American School of Classical Studies at Athens provided the first evidence that we have for one of the major harbors of ancient Greece.

Five seasons of work at the site brought to light a cross section of life in a once-bustling Roman port. At first we had hoped to find a Greek harbor city and, indeed, modest remains of the classical and Hellenistic periods appeared here and there in the area. Principally, however, the Kenchreai we dug was a Roman city, refounded in the mid-1st century B.C.E., along with its mother city, Corinth, by Julius Caesar and built up by his heir, the later emperor Augustus. Roman policy had seen to the destruction of Corinth in 146 B.C.E. and the sites of the city and its twin harbors had lain virtually abandoned for over 100 years.

Little was known about Kenchreai before our work began. The Apostle Paul took a ship east from there once and even recorded the name of a deaconess of the local Christian community, one Phoebe, to whom local tradition attributed a church-like structure whose foundations have always been visible just breaking the surface of the sea by the south mole of the ancient harbor. The 2nd-century writer, Apuleius, set the climax of his famous novel *The Golden Ass* in the sanctuary of Isis at Kenchreai. His contemporary, the travel writer Pausanias, told of this sanctuary and another of Aphrodite at the ends of the harbor moles. The harbor itself appeared on coins of the mid-2nd century emperor Antonius Pius, perhaps commemorating imperial benefactions in Corinth and her territory. Visible at the end of the north mole are still massive blocks that supported a colossal bronze statue of Poseidon that also appears on this coin. Otherwise, like many other towns in Rome's broad empire, Kenchreai lived for centuries in anonymous prosperity.

By the early 5th century C.E., a Christian church replaced the pagan sanctuary of Isis and in the late 6th century the site was mostly abandoned as Slavic raiders swept into Greece. Small quantities of medieval pottery and coins attest a modest medieval presence, and it may be that Byzantine and Crusader armies and traders still made use of the dilapidated harbor installations. Soon even they were gone, as Greece settled into four centuries of Turkish domination. History again touched the site briefly during World War II, when Italian defenses for the nearby Corinth Canal were carved out of the North Hill above the harbor; a legacy of this period was a mine field discovered during the first season of excavation, happily without explosive consequences.

Our work concentrated on three areas in particular, with some minor investigations elsewhere on the site: along the landward ends of the south and north moles and underwater in the harbor. The most important area examined lay by the south mole beside the modern road that cuts through the site. In this area we recovered a succession of religious buildings, pagan and Christian, whose contents are among the most remarkable ever found in Greece. Interesting, too, was the seaside by the north mole, where a large Roman brick building, with walls still three meters high in places, perhaps marked the site of Aphrodite's sanctuary. The hill above this structure proved to be honeycombed with underground Roman tombs, some still preserving traces of paintings on their walls, one leading into another through ancient robbers' cuttings like veritable catacombs.

Roman Corinth, like her Greek predecessor, became one of the great trading cities of the eastern Mediterranean and Kenchreai cargoes came and went down the watery ways to the rich cities of Asia Minor, Cyprus, Syria, and Egypt. One of the earliest structures of the newly founded town seems to have been the harbor installations: two moles made up of hundreds of thousands of cubic meters of dumped rubble ran out 100 meters from the shore to provide a sheltered anchorage; on the south one a line of warehouses stretching at least 200 meters along the mole and inland housed exports and imports. At its outer end was a complex of small, interconnected tanks that indicate a piscina, a holding area for fresh fish for the tables of the well-to-do. Land subsidence over the past 1,400 years has resulted in the modern sea level being at least a meter and a half higher than in antiquity, effectively drowning most of these remains and leaving the surface of the moles under water.

An important aspect of our work was excavating underwater deposits along the mole; in particular, we located an enormous dump of the 1st and early 2nd centuries C.E., where the garbage of the harbor side seems to have been deposited for over a century. Slow and painstaking excavation over two seasons enabled us to uncover a small part of this deposit, some two meters deep, down to clean sand. Under the direction of Professor Joseph Shaw (now of the University of Toronto), our work at Kenchreai marked a pioneering effort at shallow-water excavation in Greece and demonstrated that it was possible to dig stratigraphically under water and to recover finds that could help date adjacent structures.

The most striking finds under water did not, however, come from our divers' work, but rather from an apse-ended structure visible at the landward end of the south mole (Area A). Initial work in the area on land had uncovered a Christian church of the 5th–6th centuries with many associated burials, but below it were traces of a long corridor that led into the water to the apse. A floor that was almost level with the sea covered the structure, but removing it revealed a broad flight of stairs running down into the water. Pumps were put to work night and day to remove the water while sand bags and plastic sheeting kept the waves at bay. What emerged was totally unexpected: a series of over 100 glass panels in the remains of their original wooden packing cases, sealed into the building about 370 C.E. after a great earthquake and possible tidal wave in the Corinthiad. Removal, consolidation, and study of these panels posed numerous problems, some that continue to this day, but the result was to add a chapter to the history of late Roman art.

The panels were made up of cut pieces of glass—a technique called opus sectile, previously known only in marble—set in decorative patterns into a pitch matrix backed with large pieces of broken pottery for stability. A bewildering variety of scenes emerged as the panels were cleaned and separated: exotic landscapes with crocodiles, magnificent buildings lining a sea front, ships great and small, a variety of sea life, and a powerful, almost Byzantine image of a bearded man on a pedestal, who was conveniently labelled "Homeros." Later, two other male figures, the philosophers Plato and Theophrastos, also appeared, along with a variety of geometric decorative shapes. It is likely that these panels had been imported from Alexandria in Egypt to line the entrance hall of a religious sanctuary, almost certainly that of Isis. The later 4th century was not a happy time for the pagan religions of the Roman Empire, as the newly official Christian religion established itself. However, for a brief period during the reign of Julian (361–6 C.E.), the old ways were again encouraged and it seems reasonable to associate our opus sectile with a refitting of the sanctuary at that time. But the panels never seem to have left their packing cases (unless in fact they were being repacked for shipment elsewhere) and the death of Julian and a devastating earthquake in 365 C.E. made them redundant and the whole complex, mosaic floor and fountain, were filled in and later incorporated into the church.

Across the harbor another major area of excavation revealed an impressive Roman brick building of the early 2nd century C.E. with some later remodeling, much of which had been washed away by the sea (Area C). What remains is a well-constructed complex of rooms around a colonnaded courtyard. Mosaic floors adorned some of the rooms and the walls were once covered with fine marble panels and perhaps frescoes. The purpose of the structure is uncertain, but it seems a likely candidate for the Aphrodiseion mentioned by Pausanias near the north mole. Such shrines to the goddess of love often took a different form from the usual Greco-Roman temple—especially at Corinth, a city notorious for its courtesans—and a number of erotically decorated fragments of pottery and clay lamps suggests amorous interests on the part of the occupants. Recent excavations at Mytilene near its north harbor have revealed a similar Roman building right in the middle of the modern town's red-light district. Of course, it is possible that it could have been some other sort of public building, like the harbor master's offices, but excavations in it also uncovered scores of bone hairpins that suggest a sizable number of ladies in the household.

Scattered trenches in other areas of the site revealed scrappy bits of Kenchreai's history. It is likely that the Greek site lay some distance to the west, perhaps in part under a modern army base near our site, and that silting up of the original harbor, possibly visible in aerial photographs as a wedge-shaped area running inland, resulted in the Romans developing a new one. The only clear traces of the pre-Roman town appeared on top of a hill north of the harbor (Area G), where a number of vats and a variety of loom weights suggest a center for cloth production and dyeing. Sections of the classical-Hellenistic city wall are still visible in this area, too. Further north from the harbor, a chance discovery in 1963 led to the excavation of a monumental early Roman tomb that once dominated the skyline here above the sea. A fragmentary inscription suggests that it was built by a prominent local family in the first century C.E.

Another result of our excavations was the possibility of studying 600 years' accumulation of the pottery, coins, and bric-a-brac of daily life at a cosmopolitan port. Apart from a sprinkling of earlier Greek and later medieval material, most of what we found belongs to the Roman and early Byzantine town. As one might expect there was a wide variety of imported material: pottery and oil lamps from Italy in the early years of the town's new life give way to imports from Asia Minor and to local products as well as those of Athens as the centuries rolled by. Even more distant destinations such as Cyprus, Syria, and Egypt are represented.

The lamps are of particular interest, as for many years manufacturers placed small scenes in relief on the circular tops of these simple lighting devices. On Kenchreai lamps we find depicted, for example, the emperors Augustus and Hadrian, various gods and goddesses, scenes of daily life, including a variety of erotic symplegmata, gladiators, and actors. During the 2nd century C.E., the lamp shops of Corinth produced some of the finest ones ever made in the ancient world.

The coins also have a story to tell: over 1,300 of them were more or less datable and illustrate the changing history and fortunes of the city. About 10 percent were pre-Roman, from the 4th to mid-2nd centuries B.C.E., and all the rest were Roman to medieval. A silver coin of Mark Antony attests activity early after the city's refounding, while the presence of several hoards of coins, perhaps buried for safekeeping, demonstrates the end of Kenchreai as a flourishing early Byzantine town about 580 C.E., as the Slavs and Avars poured into Greece from the north. Thereafter, only about 50 coins can be identified from the next 800 years that saw Byzantine rule eventually give way to Frankish and Venetian, until the coming of the Turks ended all visible activity at our site.

REFERENCES

Adamshek, B.
1979 *Kenchreai. The Pottery*. Vol. 4. Leiden.
Hohlfelder, R. L.
1978 *Kenchreai. The Coins.* Vol. 3. Leiden.
Ibrahim, L., R. L. Scranton and R. Brill
1976 *Kenchreai. The Panels of Opus Sectile in Glass.* Vol. 2. Leiden.
Scranton, R. L., J. W. Shaw and L. Ibrahim
1978 *Kenchreai. Topography and Architecture.* Vol. 1. Leiden.
Scranton, R. L.
Kenchreai. The Inscriptions. Vol. 6. (Forthcoming) Leiden.
Thimme, D. and W. Stern
Kenchreai. The Small Finds. Vol. 7. (Forthcoming) Leiden.
Williams, E. H.
1981 *Kenchreai. The Lamps.* Vol. 5. Leiden.

CARL DARLING BUCK

Eric Pratt Hamp

CARL Darling Buck (1866–1955), who served in the first quarter of this century on the executive committee of the Chicago Society of the Archaeological Institute of America, was one of the 29 persons who announced the need for an organization which became in 1924 the Linguistic Society of America, and was twice the president of that society within the first 15 years of its existence. Buck was not a linguist in the sense of many present-day scholars of that discipline, because his primary interest was not in the abstract properties of the general build of human language, the generalizations of syntax and grammar and systems of sounds that may be stated for human languages at large (or even artificial or synthesized or programmed languages today). However, such aspirations were not foreign to him: his last major book (1949, and reprinted just two years ago) was a vast attempt to study notional categories expressed in the meanings of forms represented in the lexical stock of most branches of the Indo-European language family, from which Buck hoped that we might ultimately with sufficient further study deduce important principles of semantic change and the growth of ideas.

Among linguists Buck is to be classed as a philologist and historical comparativist working in the Indo-European language family, and especially on the terrain of Greece and Italy, in the heart of the tradition that flowered in the later nineteenth century, and which historians of that discipline call neogrammarian, translating the term Junggrammatiker, which was applied to the avant garde theoreticians who developed such views in Germany during the 1870s and 1880s—just the period of Buck's education and formation and the period whose centenary we are celebrating today. Buck's training and his great life work were dedicated to the exploration of the known historical development over the past few millenia and the prehistory, reconstructed for a time span before the advent of writing and the documentation we consequently possess, of the Indo-European family of languages and the descendants that we call Greek and Italic. If we recognize William Dwight Whitney of Yale as the first great modern linguist and comparativist of this country, with his renowned and influential studies of the general nature of language, of language change, of the lexical store of English, and most of all with his monumental and still definitive grammatical account of Sanskrit, we must place Carl Darling Buck as chronologically the second American in this category and noble tradition, and as the primary intellectual channel for later American scholarship in this philological mode. With the exception of the important American anthropological vein and a slender but formative later contribution from the logicians and formalizers, Buck's contribution accounts for nearly everything that has become powerful in American theorizing in the field of linguistics today.

Buck was a philologist, and remained a philologist of classical studies and Indo-European comparativism all his life. He was trained in his early youth, not unusually, in the classics along with his liberal arts education, but at an early point he both excelled and received outstanding scholarly guidance. He came from a background that valued learning and hard work. It was therefore a convergence of happy factors that led him to enter Yale early, to pursue serious studies in the classics, to begin Sanskrit in his senior year with the head of his intellectual pedigree, Whitney, and to travel while still a student in Greece for study and direct experience. Buck's formation fated him to become the pivotal scholarly figure that he was. His hiring by President Harper immediately upon the completion of his studies when the University of Chicago opened its doors in 1892, brought to Chicago and to scholarship in classics and to the formation of this Chicago Society a major personage who was still at a vigorously young and productive age. Chicago was assured instantly of a uniquely rich resource that made Chicago in this sense a central point for the national development over the next third of a century in the disciplines that Buck dominated.[1]

All his life Buck remained intensely interested in archaeology, and in his active work in the philological interpretation of Greek and the Italic dialects made constant use of archaeological findings, particularly from the epigraphic point of view that lay necessarily at the basis of his magisterial work with inscriptions, a lasting aspect of his scholarship, which all the world utilizes today. While still a

---

1 In this brief presentation we must forego the details of Buck's biography, but an excellent contentive obituary by Buck's distinguished Indo-Europeanist student (the first major American specialist in Tocharian philology and linguistics), George Sherman Lane, is available in *Language* 31 (1955): 181–90; and the present writer, who knew the awesome figure of Buck as a beginning instructor from 1950 until his death, published an invited obituary in ΠΛΑΤΩΝ 1957. A detailed and precise bibliography of Buck's scholarly writings by Vittoria Mondolfo was published in *Language* 32 (1956): 603–7. That bibliography forms the basis for the summarizing statements made below.

student, in association with the American School of Classical Studies, in Greece, Buck engaged in archaeological activity that resulted in his doctoral dissertation (1889) at Yale on *The Choregia in Athens and at Ikaria* and in nine papers during 1888–89 (together with his teacher Frank B. Tarbell; cf. his obituary of Tarbell in *Classical Philology* 16 (1921): 95) on Anthedon and on the Attic deme of Ikaria, embracing many matters other than just the inscriptions, published both in the *Papers of the American School* and in the *AJA*. Buck's interest in archaeology also embraced a visit to Egypt, where according to his notebook he took part at this time in his studies in some excavations. It is also recorded that during his stay in Greece he went on a walking tour of the Pelopónnesos; although I never heard Buck speak Greek, these contacts doubtless formed his lifelong sympathy with the serious study and mastery of Modern Greek, an attitude not commonly found among serious classical scholars of his day. Buck had experience on the ground with the classical archaeology that he so deeply respected, and can rightly be called a professional archaeologist even though his later busy life absorbed all his active working time in the pursuits of philology and language.

We have seen that Buck's pedigree in his American education was second to none in its patrician antecedents. After Buck's first studies in Europe, which he visited on later occasions in his scholarly life, and his doctorate at Yale and subsequent marriage, and before his acceptance of the position at the University of Chicago, where he spent all his distinguished active career and retirement, the next phase of his remarkable intellectual heritage came into place: Buck returned to Germany with the thought of studying Indo-Iranian philology and linguistics with the great Vedic scholar Karl Geldner. He went to Leipzig, and then followed Geldner for a year to Berlin, whither the latter had moved. After that, Buck returned to Leipzig and studied under Karl Brugmann and August Leskien as well as others there. Both of these scholars are names absolutely at the pinnacle of Junggrammatiker fame and innovation, Brugmann a great Greek scholar and the synthesizer of our fundamental knowledge of Indo-European as we still understand it today, even after the subsequent discovery of Hittite, Tocharian, and other less crucial new findings; Leskien was a great Slavist and Lithuanian scholar whose fundamental statement laid the basis of Junggrammatiker theory that guides us still today. This is a superb heritage. Berlin and Leipzig were at odds in the theoretical debate of the time, and it is a mark of Buck's sure acumen and judgment that he chose to return to Leipzig. His pedigree was now complete and the ensuing period at Chicago was a fulfillment and ornament to our learning.

Buck's published works form an enviably solid and remarkable record. Though he thought at first to follow Whitney in Sanskritic and Iranian (Avestan and Old Persian) learning, he published just two titles on Sanskrit and five on older Iranian, all early in his career except for one on an inscription of Darius in 1927. On Latin, of which he was an acknowledged master, he published a well-known grammar (1903) together with William Gardner Hale [whose obituary he wrote in *Classical Philology* 23 (1928): 278–9] and eight shorter pieces. Buck's name is associated the world over with the Italic dialects on which he published two books (1892, offered for a prize for which he was technically unqualified, as it turned out; and 1904, reprinted 1928, translated 1905). We see, however, where the lion's share of his work went: three great and lasting books (1910, totally revised 1955, weeks after his death; and a superb, indispensable item 1944) and 55 shorter items on Greek. There are also two publications on Modern Greek. All students and many scholars of the world still today constantly use the reprinting of his comparative Greek and Latin textbook (1933). The crowning achievement of his Indo-European publication, on which he gave us 15 shorter studies, is the book published in 1949.

Single items were also published on Old English, Hittite, Balkan philology, English etymology, language in its distribution in Europe and the development of nations, the theory of text criticism, the linguistic situation in ancient Italy and Greece, and in Greece of the second millenium B.C.E.—a career of vast production still serving us today, a career of broad learning, yet of sharp, well-defined focus, a career devoted unswervingly to our knowledge of the ancient Aegean and to Italy outside of Rome as well.

Three years before his statutory retirement in 1933, Buck was honored by appointment as the Martin A. Ryerson Distinguished Service Professor for Sanskrit and Comparative Philology. The name of Carl Darling Buck is justly celebrated in the title of an endowed University of Chicago professorial chair.

REFERENCES

Buck, C. D.

1904 *A Grammar of Oscan and Umbrian, with a Collection of Inscriptions and a Glossary*. Boston.

1910 *Introduction to the Study of Greek Dialects: Grammar, Selected Inscriptions. Glossary*. Boston, New York.

1933 *Comparative Grammar of Greek and Latin*. Chicago.

1949 *A Dictionary of Selected Synonyms in the Principal Indo-European Languages: A Contribution to the History of Ideas*. Chicago.

Buck, C. D. and W. G. Hale

1903 *A Latin Grammar*. Boston.

Buck, C. D. and W. Petersen
1944 *A Reverse Index of Greek Nouns and Adjectives Arranged by Terminations*. Chicago.

Lane, G. S.
1955 Carl Darling Buck (Obituary Notice). *Language: Journal of the Linguistic Society of America* 31: 2 (1955) 181–90.

Mondolfo, V.
1955 Notes (a full bibliography of Carl Darling Buck's writings). *Language: Journal of the Linguistic Society of America* 32: 3 (1956) 603–07.

CHICAGO MUSEUMS AND THE CHICAGO SOCIETY

Eleanor Guralnick

EXCAVATION holds the romance of archaeology, but it is not the whole of archaeology. The Chicago Society of the AIA has been sustained for 100 years largely by professional members whose contribution to archaeology has been in the study and analysis of artifacts excavated by others. Many of these artifacts could also be defined by the term "objects of art." An object with aesthetic value often has enhanced value as an archaeological artifact. It may play an important role enlarging our understanding of the culture, values, and technology of the peoples who made it.

Founders and leaders of the Chicago Society took on the critical responsibilities for establishing the major Chicago museum collections of ancient art and artifacts. All of the individuals named below shared commitments to museums and universities together with lifelong commitments to the Chicago Society of the Archaeological Institute of America.

Charles A. Hutchinson was president of the Art Institute of Chicago. He and the director of the museum, William M. R. French, assembled the core of the present Classical Collection.

Edward Everett Ayer was largely responsible for the creation of the Classical and Egyptological collections of the Field Museum of Natural History. It was he who located the Tomb of Unis Anhk, now the centerpiece of the present Ancient Egypt exhibit at that museum. The persuasive Edward Ayer convinced Marshall Field to fund the establishment of that museum.

Martin A. Ryerson, a founding and life member of the Chicago Society, purchased the Tomb of Unis Anhk for the Field Museum. A philanthropist and chairman of the Board of Trustees of the University of Chicago, he generously gave many objects of ancient art to the Art Institute and contributed his private library of books on art and archaeology to establish the Martin A. Ryerson Library at that museum. His gifts to the University of Chicago included many books on classical art and archaeology, which are now in the Regenstein Library Special Collections. Generations of archaeology students at the University of Chicago have benefited from his generosity in establishing scholarships and fellowships for study, travel, and research on the archaeology of the lands of the ancient Mediterranean.

Alfred Emerson was one of the very first Professors of Classics at the University of Chicago. Shortly thereafter as the first curator of the Classical Collection of the Art Institute of Chicago, he published the first catalogue of these antiquities in 1889.

James H. Breasted, the University of Chicago's first Professor of Egyptology, conceived the idea of the Oriental Institute as an institute with museum, research, and educational functions. He developed the museum collections with both excavated materials and purchased objects. Many of the most splendid artifacts in the Oriental Institute were acquired through Breasted's efforts. His broad interests allowed him to publish articles about groups of or single objects as well as the more general histories for which he is well known.

Frank Bigelow Tarbell was the University of Chicago's first Professor of Classical Archaeology, appointed in 1892. Nearly all of his scholarly work related to classical art. His museum studies, which were published often in the *American Journal of Archaeology* or *Studies in Classical Philology*, included such titles as "A Signed Kylix by Duris," "A Greek Hand Mirror in the Art Institute of Chicago," "A Kantharos from the Factory of Brygos," and "Architecture on Attic Vases." His books included *A History of Greek Art* and *A Catalogue of Bronzes in the Field Museum of Natural History*. Tarbell believed that teaching was enhanced by having close on hand genuine examples of artifacts. He brought together the core of the collection of ancient artifacts now in the David and Alfred Smart Gallery of the University of Chicago. The first substantial acquisition was from Mr. E. P. Warren, a collector who gave gifts to many U.S. museums. William Gardner Hale, University of Chicago Classics Department Chairman, contributed a collection of prehistoric potsherds, which he had acquired from Heinrich Schliemann. In more recent years, the collection of Carl Darling Buck was presented to the gallery by his daughter-in-law. Buck was a Professor of Indo-European Linguistics at the University of Chicago for over 40 years.

Franklin Plotinus Johnson came to the University of Chicago by 1925 as Professor of Archaeology following the retirement of Tarbell. Classical art was his special interest, following the tradition established by Tarbell during his many years as Professor of Archaeology. Johnson's early work included his *Foundations for a Study of Lysippus*, and within two more years, in 1927, his book on *Lysippus*, which was reissued in 1968. A couple of years later, Johnson wrote the volume on *Sculpture 1896–1923, Corinth*, Vol. IX. The AIA published his monograph on *The Farwell Collection*. In addition, he studied the vases that are now in the collection of the Smart Gallery and those in the Art Institute of Chicago, with many publications in the *American Journal of Archaeology* and the *Art Bulletin* resulting.

Peter von Blanckenhagen has received the Archaeological Institute of America's highest honor, its gold medal, in recognition of a lifetime of outstanding contributions to archaeology. Much of his work is related to the analysis and interpretation of works of classical art.

The tradition of scholarship in classical art has continued down to the present. Robert L. Scranton's *Aesthetic Aspects of Ancient Art* suggest an extraordinary view of the arts of the ancient civilizations surrounding the eastern Mediterranean. Raymond V. Schoder, S.J., gave us an illuminating picture of the Greek world in his *Greece from the Air*. He created an extraordinary resource in his slide photographs of classical archaeological sites and of art from museums in both eastern and western Europe and elsewhere around the world. He made this extraordinary resource available to the Archaeological Institute of America, allowing copies to be acquired by universities everywhere. Kathleen Shelton works exclusively with Late Roman and Early Christian art. Ira Mark enjoyed the special privilege of reexcavating the Nike Apteros sanctuary high on the Athenian acropolis as he developed a complete picture of its sculptural friezes. Still others closely associated with leadership within the society, Louise Berge, Joan Haldenstein, and Robert Sutton, study Greek vase painting. James Packer has dug through the storerooms of the Basilica Ulpia in Rome to prepare the first complete study of that architectural monument, the largest public building of ancient Rome. I have devoted much of my time to studies of Greek sculpture and to investigations of interconnections between the art of Greece and that of Egypt and the Near East as illuminated by excavated artifacts now in museum collections.

The sense of nonprofessional members of the Chicago Society of the signal importance of museums to the life of the community led Julius Rosenwald, a lifelong member, to establish the Museum of Science and Industry of Chicago. Whereas its main function is in other areas of public education, that museum has a collection of ancient artifacts, mainly tools and coins, that illustrate the history of technology.

One of the very earliest members, Harlow N. Higinbotham, found an outlet for his very strong commitment to broad public education by organizing for success the 1892 World's Columbian Exposition. As president of the event, he planned the exhibits to emphasize both the industrial and artistic achievements of man. The success of that mammoth enterprise was largely thanks to his efforts.

To illustrate the degree of devotion that some leaders offered the Chicago Society—Frank Wakely Gunsaulus was willing to undertake to be simultaneously president of the Armour Institute (forerunner of the Illinois Institute of Technology) and of the Chicago Society. A scholar of the history of art, he lectured to the Chicago Society on Persian ceramics on two separate occasions, and was the first to illustrate his talk with slides made by color photography in 1914.

The Chicago Society of the Archaeological Institute of America was founded in order to further archaeological excavation. The earliest record of the society tells us specifically that the formation of the Chicago Society was invited to strengthen the national organization sufficiently to enable it to undertake the excavation of the Sanctuary of Apollo at Delphi. Although the French took on that responsibility, the Chicago Society independently sponsored the archaeological exploration of Cyrene for three seasons, 1910, 1911, and 1912. Nevertheless, during the past hundred years the energies of its founders were engaged in the development of museum collections, and many of its leaders among the professional archaeologists, were devoted to the study and interpretation of artifacts excavated by others.

REFERENCES

Adamshek, B.

1969 *Roman Pottery in the Field Museum of Natural History.* Master's thesis. University of Chicago.

Johnson, F. P.

1925 *Foundations for a Study of Lysippos.* Chicago.

1927 *Lysippos.* Chicago.

1931 *Sculpture 1896–1923. Corinth* 9. Cambridge, Massachusetts.

1937 Oltos and Euphronios, *Art Bulletin*: 537–60.

1938 Red Figured Pottery at Chicago. *AJA* 42: 345–60.

1943 Black Figured Pottery at Chicago. *AJA* 47: 385–402.

1943 A Pelike Painted by Hermonax, *Classical Studies in Honor of William Abbott Oldfather.*

1949 Eight Pieces of Pottery. *AJA* 53: 245–47.

1953 *The Farwell Collection.* New York.

Scranton, R. L.

1964 *Aesthetic Aspects of Ancient Art.* Chicago.

Tarbell, F. B.
1895 Direction of Writing in Attic Vase Inscriptions, *Studies in Classical Philology* I.
1900 A Signed Kylix by Duris. *AJA* 4.
1901 A Greek Hand Mirror in the Art Institute of Chicago. *AJA* 5.
1902 A Kantharos from the Factory of Brygos. *AJA* 6.
1902 *A History of Greek Art.* Chicago.
1909 *A Catalogue of Bronzes, etc., in the Field Museum of Natural History in Chicago.* 8 vols. Chicago.
1910 Architecture on Attic Vases. *AJA* 14.

Zacharias, H. J.
1948 *Seven Terracottas in the Classical Collection of the University of Chicago.* Master's thesis. University of Chicago.

LIST OF ABBREVIATIONS

AB	*Art Bulletin*
AJA	*American Journal of Archaeology*
BASOR	*Bulletin*, American Schools for Oriental Research
BibO	*Bibliotheca Orientalis*
Isthmia	*University of Chicago Excavations at Isthmia*
JARCE	*Journal*, American Research Center in Egypt
JEA	*Journal of Egyptian Archaeology*
Kenchreai	*Kenchreai, Eastern Port of Corinth*
LB	Late Bronze Age
MB	Middle Bronze Age
NARCE	*Newsletter*, American Research Center in Egypt
OIP	*Oriental Institute Publications*

LIST OF ILLUSTRATIONS

FIGURES

Fig. 13 Ruins of Migdal at Shechem, of Middle Bronze IIc date, with the top of the fortifications of the same date in the foreground. View looks southeast toward Balatah.

Fig. 14 Standing stone remounted in its socle, from Shechem Late Bronze temple forecourt.

Fig. 15 Ruins of Shechem's East Gate of Middle Bronze IIc date (ca. 1600–1540 B.C.E.). G. Ernest Wright at the top of the steps points toward orthostats. Interior of the city is in the foreground.

Fig. 16 View toward the north and Shechem Tell (left center) from the flanks of Mt. Girizim, with the modern village of Balatah covering its southern half. Slopes of Ebal are at upper left. Shechem plain stretches east and south.

Fig. 17 Map of Galilee showing Upper and Lower Galilee and some key sites. Hammath Tiberias (not pictured) is immediately south of Tiberias.

Fig. 18 Mosaic floor of the fourth-century synagogue at Hammath Tiberias. The floor, laid soon after 306 C.E., uses Greco-Roman artistic conventions. The central nave contains a zodiac with Helios/Sol at its center. Greek inscriptions decorate the lower panel. The stone wall across the center of the mosaic belongs to a later synagogue built over this one.

Fig. 19 Bronze altar, incense bowl, and bull found in a fourth-century cistern context at Sepphoris. According to J. F. Strange, director of the University of South Florida Excavations at Sepphoris, the bull has Serapis associations.

Fig. 20 Mosaic panel from a large peristyle house excavated during the summer of 1989 in Sepphoris Field V by the University of South Florida Excavations at Sepphoris. The mosaic of a school of Antioch workmanship had early fourth-century (Constantinian) coins on its surface.

Fig. 21 Detail of the border and acanthus decoration of the Sepphoris Field V mosaic. The repair work on the upper border, consisting of white tesserae, was done in antiquity.

Fig. 22 Detail of bird panel from the Field V house. The panel has been cut by ancient repair work visible just above the bird's head.

Fig. 23 Oscar Broneer receiving the Cross of the Taxiarchs and being inducted into the Royal Order of the Phoenix, "For Services to Greece ... predominantly for his work with the Greek War Relief." June 1961. From left to right: John Hawthorne, Mrs. Oscar Broneer, Oscar Broneer, George Wells Beadle, president of the University of Chicago, Mrs. John Hawthorne, and the Greek Consul General in Chicago.

Fig. 24 Plan of the Isthmian Sanctuary of Poseidon.

Fig. 25 Broneer measuring the statue base inscribed CEICYΦOC.

Fig. 26 Broneer with the cult statue of Amphitrite.

Fig. 27 Marble Perirrhanterion.

Fig. 28 Geometric bronze figurine.

Fig. 29 Gemstone.

Fig. 30 A battle scene drawn from a Corinthian aryballos.

Fig. 31 Plan of the harbor at Kenchreai.

Fig. 32 Plan of the fountain court and Temple of Isis.

Fig. 33 Plan of the northeast area (area C), ca. 100 C.E. (period 5).

Fig. 34 Panoramic harbor scene in glass opus sectile from Kenchreai. Panel no. 16, VI.4.B.

Fig. 35 Homeros, an idealized portrait of glass opus sectile from Kenchreai.

Fig. 36 Franklin MacVeagh, a founder and early president of the Chicago Society. The invitation of the Archaeological Institute of America to found a Chicago Society was extended to an invited group of Chicagoans at his home.

Fig. 37 Charles L. Hutchinson, a founder and first president of the Chicago Society. The founding meeting of the society was held in his home. He was the first to become a "Life Member" of the society.

Fig. 38 Edward Everett Ayer, a founder and early president of the Chicago Society. Several meetings were held in his home.

Fig. 39 Martin A. Ryerson, a founder and "Life Member" of the Chicago Society, he served on its Executive Committee from 1889 until 1925. For 30 years (1892–1922) he was chairman of the Board of Trustees of the University of Chicago.

Fig. 40 Marshall Field, one of the first members of the Chicago Society.

Fig. 41 Library of the Marshall Field House, 1905 Prairie Avenue, Chicago. The first general lecture meeting of the Chicago Society was held here.

Fig. 42 Exterior view of the Martin A. Ryerson House, 4851 Drexel Boulevard, Chicago. Several early meetings of the Chicago Society took place here.

Fig. 43 View of the archaeological exhibits of the Field Museum during the 1890s.

Fig. 44 Etruscan terra cotta ash urn. Field Museum. Gift of Edward Everett Ayer.

Fig. 45 Etruscan engraved bronze cista. Field Museum. Gift of Edward Everett Ayer.

Fig. 46 Crating the stone blocks of the Tomb of Unis Anhk for shipment from Egypt to the Field Museum. Gift of Martin A. Ryerson.

Fig. 47 The train carrying the Tomb of Unis Anhk across Egypt to point of embarcation to Chicago.

Fig. 48 Rhind Papyrus. Field Museum. Gift of Edward Everett Ayer.

Fig. 49 Attic red figure Oinochoe by the Painter of Naples 3136. The Art Institute of Chicago. Gift of Martin A. Ryerson.

Fig. 50 Attic red figure Stamnos by the Chicago Painter. The Art Institute of Chicago. Gift of Philip D. Armour and Charles L. Hutchinson.

Fig. 51 Attic black figure Pelike (Oedipus confronting the Theban Sphinx?). The Alfred and David Smart Gallery, The University of Chicago; The Frank B. Tarbell Collection.

Fig. 52 Black figure Nikosthenic Amphora fragment: Satyr's head. The Alfred and David Smart Gallery, The University of Chicago; The Frank B. Tarbell Collection.

Fig. 53 Red figure Lekanis lid fragment: Woman seated on a rock. Close to the Jena Painter. The Alfred and David Smart Gallery, The University of Chicago; The Frank B. Tarbell Collection.

Fig. 54 Nike sacrificing a bull. Molded terra cotta. The Alfred and David Smart Gallery, The University of Chicago; The Frank B. Tarbell Collection. Gift of William G. Hale, 1918.

Fig. 55 Red figure Kylix fragment. Painted by Oltos. The Alfred and David Smart Gallery, The University of Chicago; The Frank B. Tarbell Collection.

Illustrations 1 through 4 and 9 through 12 are published courtesy of the Oriental Institute of the University of Chicago.

Illustrations 13 through 16 were provided courtesy of the Drew University–McCormick Seminary–ASOR Expedition.

Illustrations 19 through 22 are published with the permission of James F. Strange.

Illustrations 43 through 48 are published courtesy of the Field Museum of Natural History.

Illustrations 49 and 50 are published courtesy of the Art Institute of Chicago.

Illustrations 51 through 55 are published courtesy of the Alfred and David Smart Gallery, The University of Chicago.

All other illustrations were provided by the authors.

Fig. 1

Fig. 2

Fig. 3

Fig. 4

BLACK SEA
CASPIAN SEA
MEDITERRANEAN SEA
PERSIAN GULF
RED SEA
R. Danube
R. Kuban
Maikop
Kostromskaya
Karmir Blur
Igdyr
R. Araxes
Tureng Tepe
Astrabad
Tepe Hissar
Amlash
Marlik
Pileh Qal'eh
Teheran
Horoztepe
Alaja Huyuk
Yazilikaya
Alishar
Boghazkoy
Ankara
Gordion
Kultepe
Altintepe
Kayalidere
Toprak Kaleh
Van
Lake Urmya
Troy
Thermi
LESBOS
Delphi
Mycenae
Tiryns
Olympia
Ephesus
Beycesultan
Hacilar
Acemhuyuk
Iflatun
Fasillar
Ivriz
Mersin
Catal Huyuk
Karatepe
Adana
Zinjirli
Sakjegozu
Malatya
Marash
Arslan Tash
Diarbekr
Harran
Birecik
Carchemish
Tell Fakhariyeh
Tell Halaf
Til Barsip
Tell Brak
Tell Rifaat
Tell Judeideh
Tavanat
Al Mina
Tell Atchana
Minet el Beida
Ras Shamra
Hama
Mishrife
Enkomi
Idalion
CYPRUS
Amathus
Curium
RHODES
Knossos
CRETE
Byblos
Beirut
Sidon
Tyre
Damascus
Tell Abu Hawwam
Megiddo
Beisan
Samaria
Jericho
Jerusalem
Ghassul
Lachish
Tell Fara
Naucratis
Heliopolis
Gizeh
Memphis
Sakkara
R. Nile
Tell el Amarna
Abydos
Tell Billa
Khorsabad
Tepe Gawra
Hasanlu
Tell Shemshara
Ziwiyeh
Sakkiz
Nineveh
Balawat
Nimrud
Tell al Rimah
Kar Tukulti-Ninurta
Jarmo
Hassuna
Assur
Nuzi
Kirkuk
Darband-i-gawr
Behistun
Ecbatana
Tepe Sialk
Kermanshah
Tepe Giyan
R. Euphrates
R. Tigris
R. Diyala
Baghouz
Samarra
Tell es Sawwan
Tell Asmar
Tell Agrab
Mari
Tell Harmal
Aqar Quf
Khafaje
Ishchali
R. Kerkha
Susa
Malamir
Masjed-i-Sulaiman
Choga Zambil
Sippar
Jemdet Nasr
Al 'Uqair
Kish
Ras al 'Amiya
Babylon
Adab
Telloh
Nippur
Umma
Isin
Fara
Warka
Larsa
Hajji Mohammed
Ur
Al 'Ubaid
Eridu
Pasargadae
Persepolis
Tall-i-Bakun
Qasr-i-Abu Nasr

Fig. 5

Fig. 6

Fig. 7

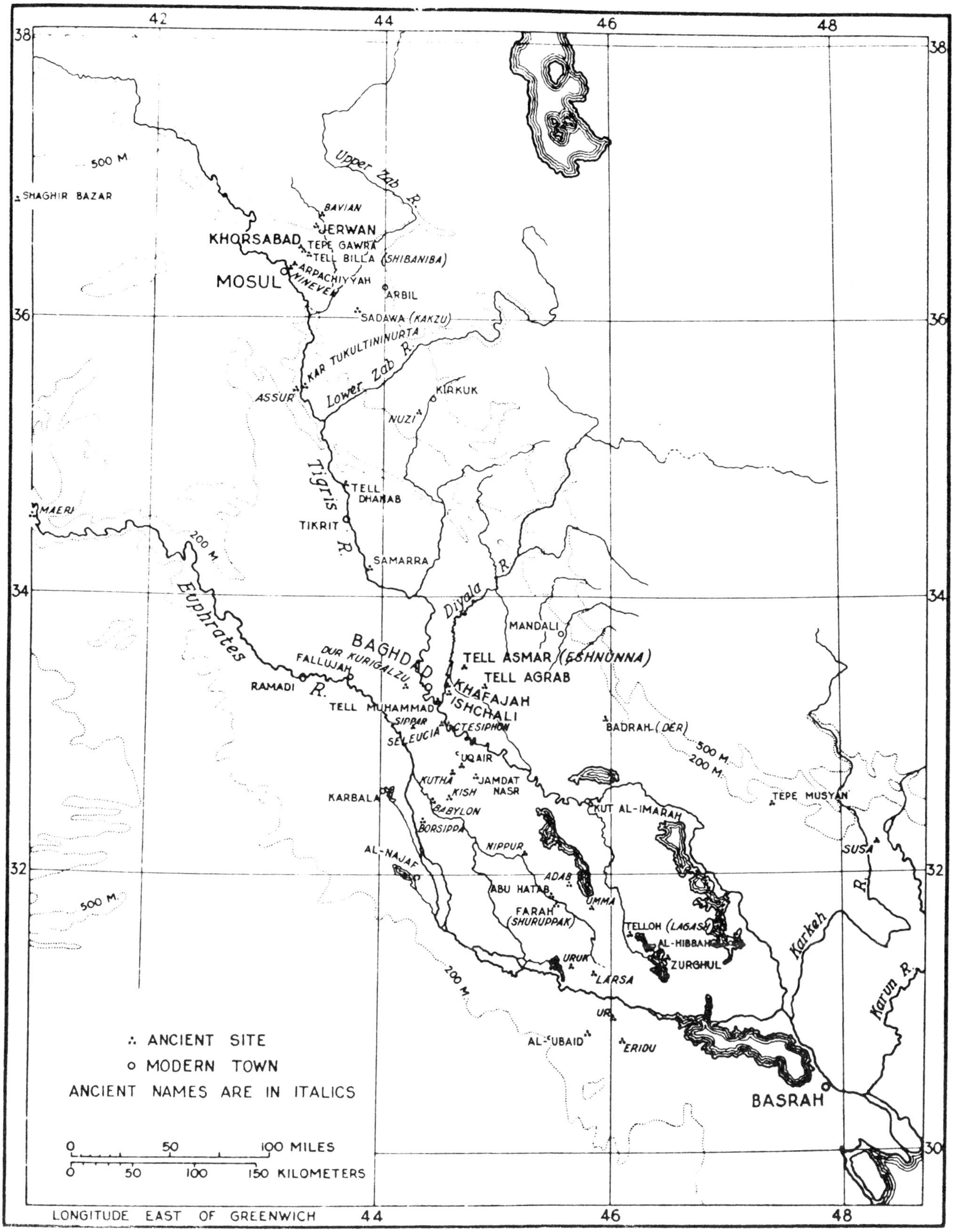

42
44
46
48
38
36
34
32
30
500 M.
SHAGHIR BAZAR
Upper Zab R.
BAVIAN
JERWAN
KHORSABAD
TEPE GAWRA
TELL BILLA (SHIBANIBA)
ARPACHIYYAH
MOSUL
NINEVEH
ARBIL
SADAWA (KAKZU)
KAR TUKULTININURTA
Lower Zab R.
ASSUR
KIRKUK
NUZI
Tigris R.
TELL DHAHAB
TIKRIT
MAERI
200 M.
SAMARRA
Euphrates R.
Diyala R.
MANDALI
BAGHDAD
DUR KURIGALZU
FALLUJAH
TELL ASMAR (ESHNUNNA)
TELL AGRAB
RAMADI
KHAFAJAH
ISHCHALI
TELL MUHAMMAD
SIPPAR
CTESIPHON
SELEUCIA
BADRAH (DER)
500 M.
200 M.
UQAIR
KUTHA
JAMDAT NASR
KISH
KARBALA
KUT AL-IMARAH
TEPE MUSYAN
BABYLON
BORSIPPA
NIPPUR
SUSA
AL-NAJAF
ADAB
R.
ABU HATAB
UMMA
500 M.
FARAH (SHURUPPAK)
TELLOH (LAGASH)
AL-HIBBAH
Karkeh
ZURGHUL
URUK
LARSA
Karun R.
200 M.
UR
AL-'UBAID
ERIDU
BASRAH
∴ ANCIENT SITE
o MODERN TOWN
ANCIENT NAMES ARE IN ITALICS
0 50 100 MILES
0 50 100 150 KILOMETERS
LONGITUDE EAST OF GREENWICH

Fig. 8

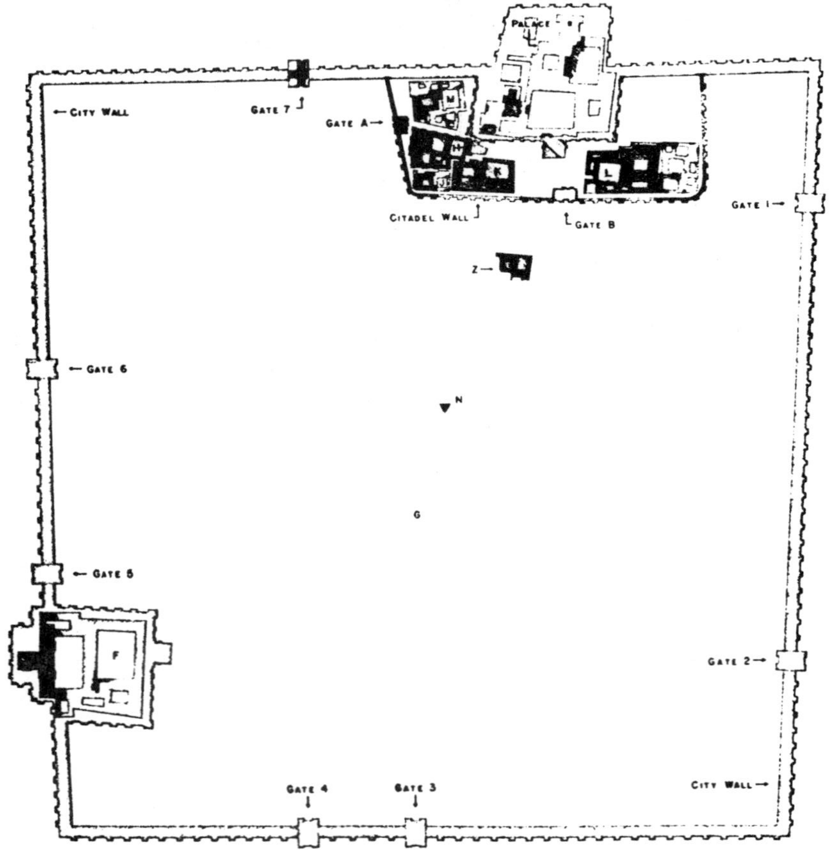
PALACE
← CITY WALL
GATE 7
GATE A →
CITADEL WALL
GATE B
GATE 1 →
Z →
N
← GATE 6
G
← GATE 5
F
GATE 2 →
GATE 4
GATE 3
CITY WALL →

Fig. 9

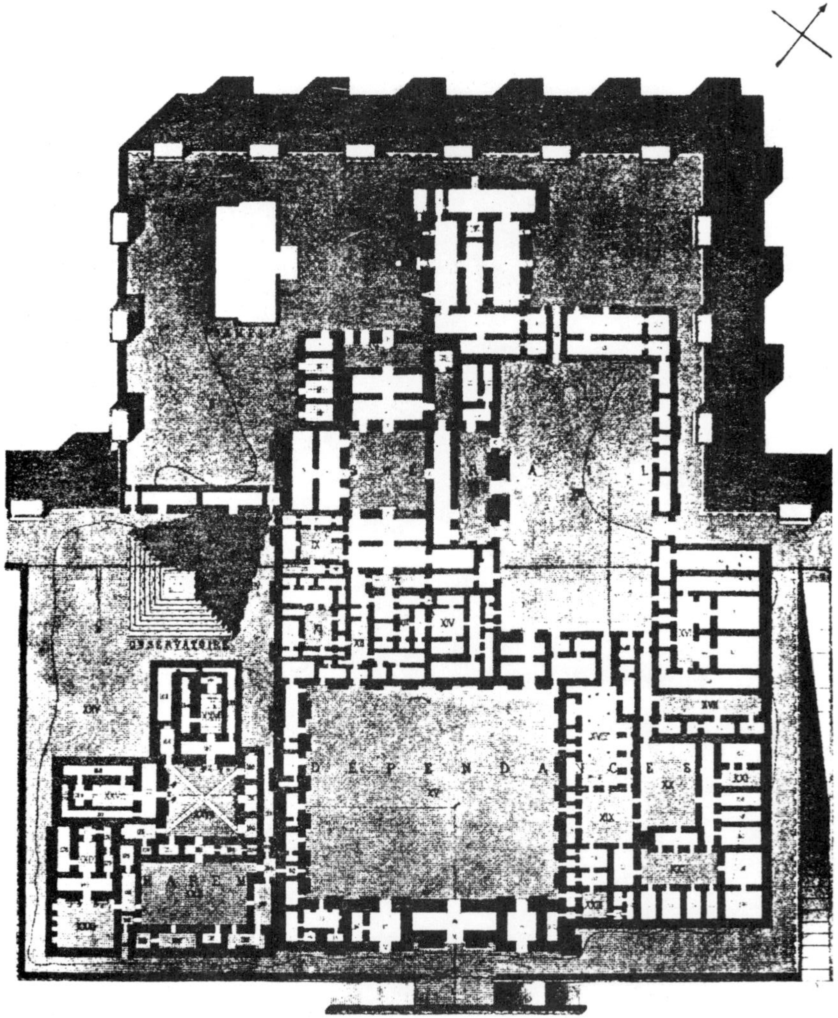
OBSERVATOIRE
DÉPENDANCES
HAREM

Fig. 10

Fig. 11

Fig. 12

Fig. 14

Fig. 15

Fig. 16

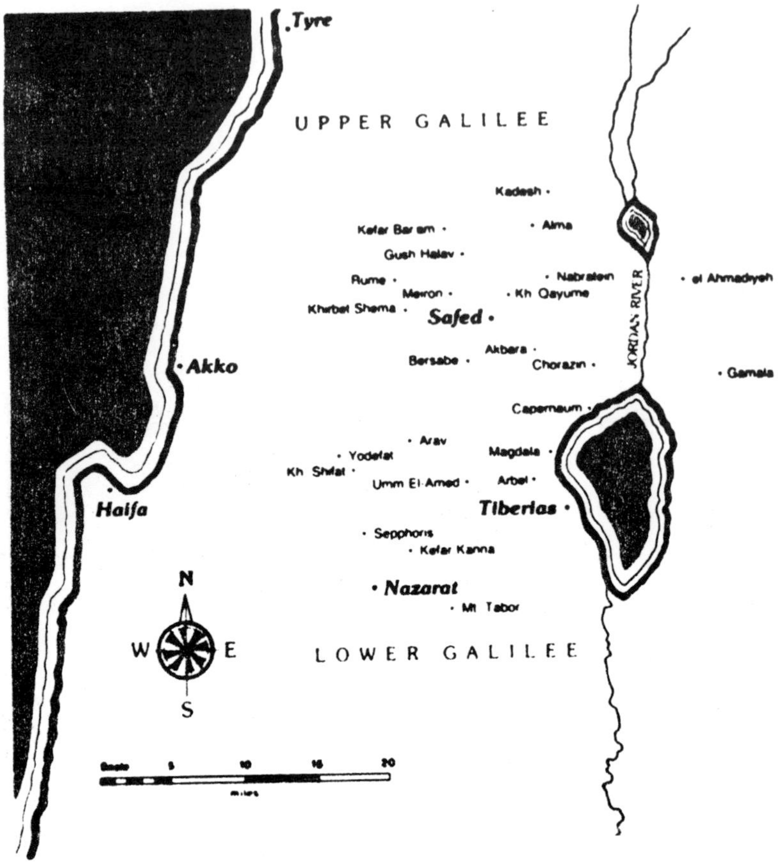
Tyre
UPPER GALILEE
Kadesh
Kefar Bar am
Alma
Gush Halav
Rume
Nabratein
el Ahmadiyeh
Meiron
Kh Qayume
Khirbet Shema
Safed
JORDAN RIVER
Akko
Akbera
Bersabe
Chorazin
Gamala
Capernaum
Arav
Yodefat
Magdala
Kh Shifat
Umm El-Amed
Arbel
Haifa
Tiberias
Sepphoris
Kefar Kanna
N
Nazarat
Mt Tabor
W
E
LOWER GALILEE
S
20

Fig. 17

Fig. 18

Fig. 19

Fig. 20

Fig. 21

Fig. 22

Fig. 23

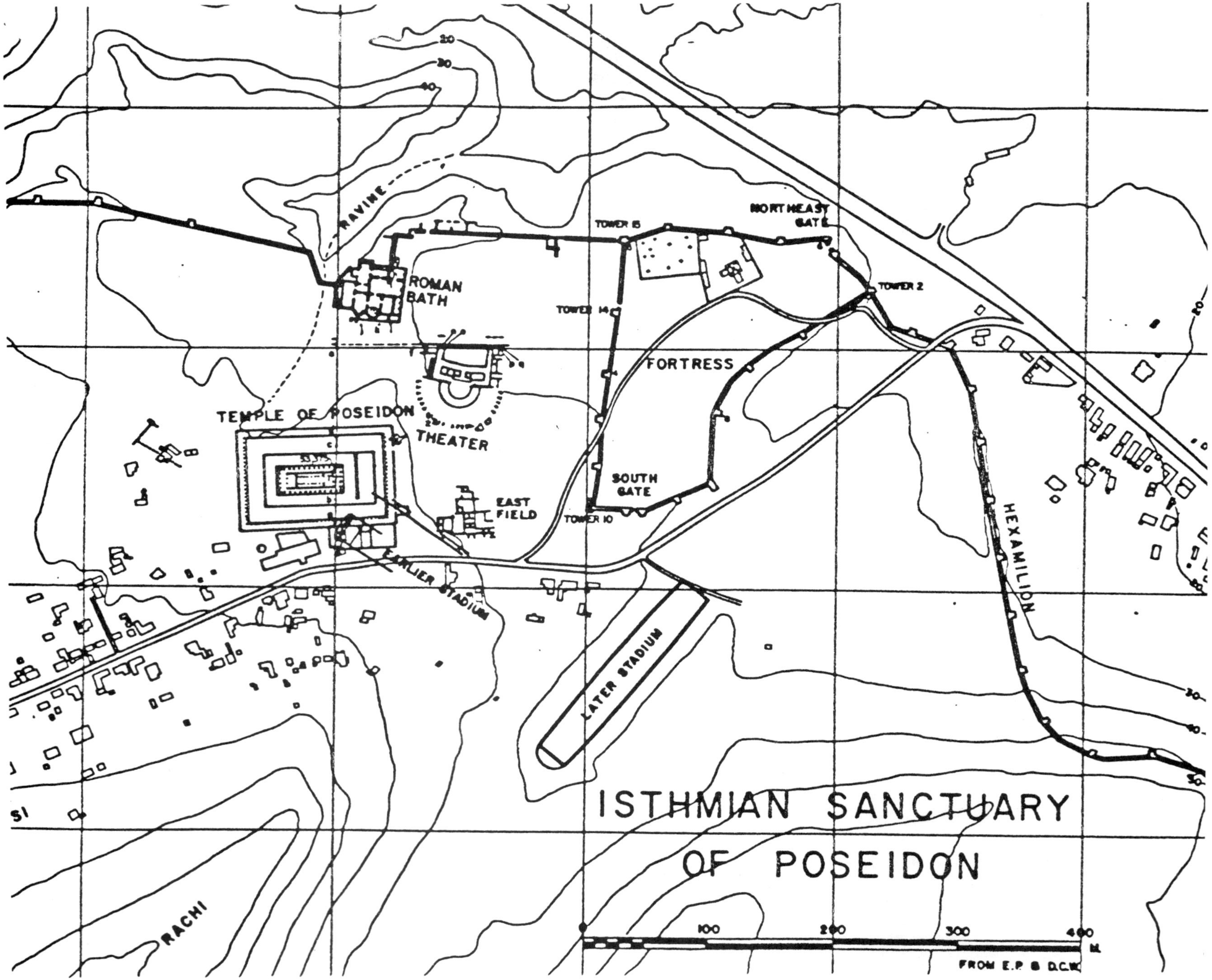
ISTHMIAN SANCTUARY
OF POSEIDON
ROMAN BATH
RAVINE
TEMPLE OF POSEIDON
THEATER
EAST FIELD
EARLIER STADIUM
LATER STADIUM
FORTRESS
SOUTH GATE
TOWER 10
TOWER 14
TOWER 15
TOWER 2
NORTHEAST GATE
HEXAMILION
RACHI
20
30
40
50
100
200
300
400
M.
FROM E.P. & D.C.W.

Fig. 25

Fig. 26

Fig. 27

Fig. 28

Fig. 29

Fig. 30

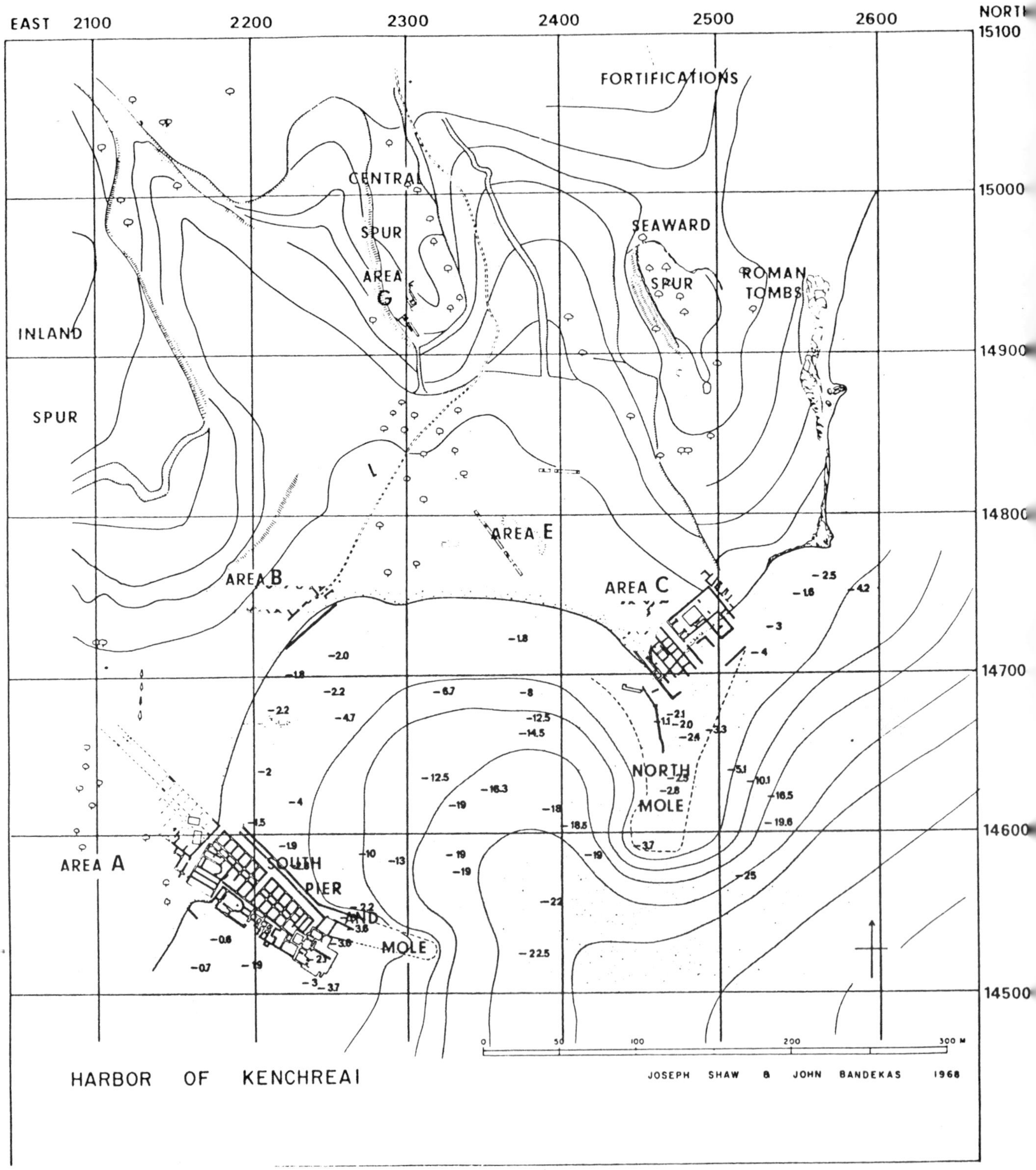
EAST 2100 2200 2300 2400 2500 2600
NORTH
15100
15000
14900
14800
14700
14600
14500
FORTIFICATIONS
CENTRAL SPUR
AREA G
SEAWARD SPUR
ROMAN TOMBS
INLAND SPUR
AREA E
AREA B
AREA C
NORTH MOLE
AREA A
SOUTH PIER AND MOLE
HARBOR OF KENCHREAI
JOSEPH SHAW & JOHN BANDEKAS 1968

Fig. 31

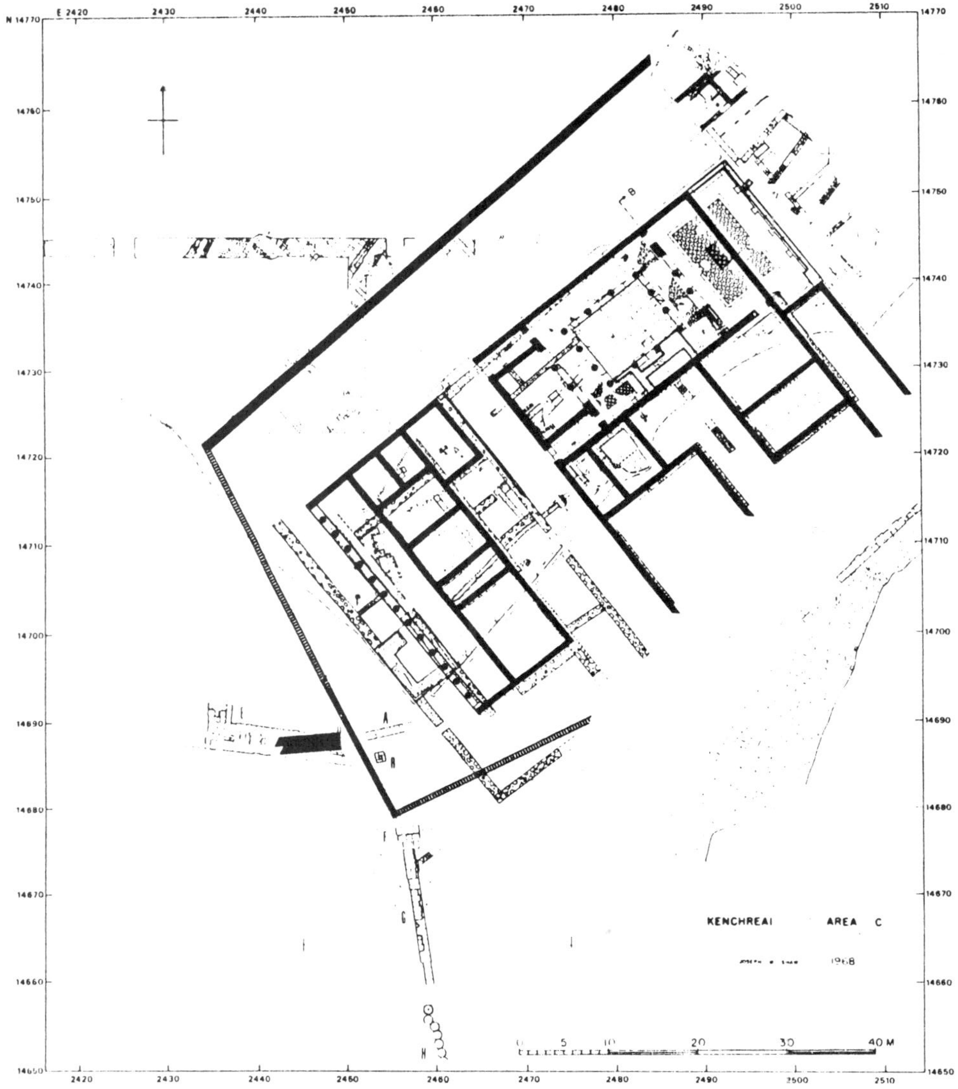

Fig. 33

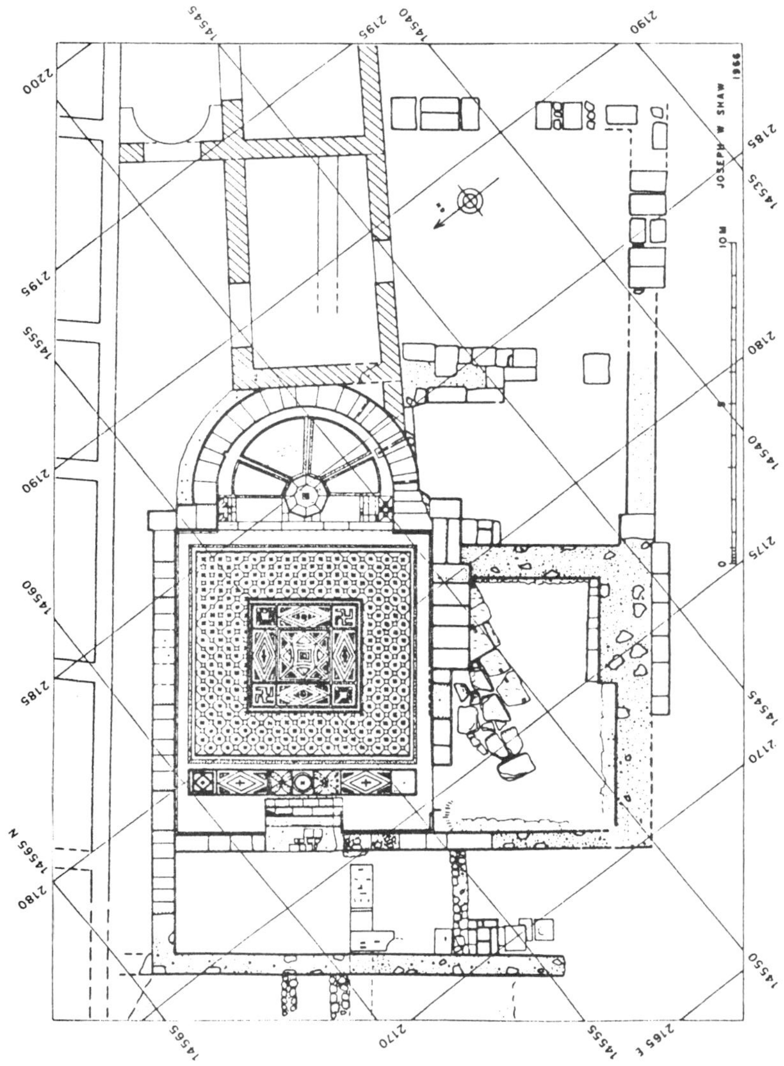

Fig. 32

Fig. 34

Fig. 35

Fig. 36

Fig. 37

Fig. 38

Fig. 39

Fig. 42

Fig. 40

Fig. 41

Fig. 43

Fig. 44

Fig. 45

Fig. 46

Fig. 47

Fig. 48

Fig. 49

Fig. 50

Fig. 51

Fig. 52

Fig. 55

Fig. 53

Fig. 54